D0048871

THE COMPLETE GUIDE TO
MINIATURE GOLDENDOODLES

David **Anderson**

Special thanks to Vanessa Richie
for her work on this project

LP Media Inc. Publishing

Text copyright © 2019 by LP Media Inc.

www.lpmedia.org

Publication Data

Anderson, David.

The Complete Guide to Miniature Goldendoodles / David Anderson. ---- First edition.

Summary: "Successfully raising a Miniature Goldendoodle dog from puppy to old age" --- Provided by publisher.

ISBN: 978-1794295360

[1. Miniature Goldendoodles --- Non-Fiction] I. Title.

This book has been written with the published intent to provide accurate and authoritative information in regard to the subject matter included. While every reasonable precaution has been taken in preparation of this book the author and publisher expressly disclaim responsibility for any errors, omissions, or adverse effects arising from the use or application of the information contained inside. The techniques and suggestions are to be used at the reader's discretion and are not to be considered a substitute for professional veterinary care. If you suspect a medical problem with your dog, consult your veterinarian.

Design by Sorin Rădulescu

First paperback edition, 2019

Cover Photo Courtesy of Jennifer Huo & Nathan Lightfoot, Photo by Sarah Dean Photography of Kansas City, MO - http://sarahdeanphotography.com/

TABLE OF CONTENTS

INTRODUCTION

Miniature Goldendoodles are one of the designer breeds with a booming popularity. Although they have only been around for a few decades, Miniature Goldendoodles have gained a reputation that is comparable to each of the breeds that make up their parentage. A lot of this admiration is due to how adorable and gregarious they are. One of the main reasons this breed has been gaining in popularity is that it is considered hypoallergenic, something that is part of the attraction to Poodles. They tend to bring many of the best characteristics of both parent breeds to make an incredibly loving and enjoyable companion with an absolutely adorable appearance.

A Miniature Goldendoodle's parents are typically a mother Golden Retriever and a father Miniature Poodle (usually about 10 inches tall and weighing 6 to 9 lbs) or Toy Poodle (around 15 inches tall and weighing 12 to 20 lbs). All of these breeds have stellar reputations for being intelligent and fantastic companions. The gentle and fun-loving personality definitely comes through in the Miniature Goldendoodle. This breed is incredibly dependent on the people who adopt them, and they love doing little more than just hanging out with their pack. If you have a smaller home, this is a fantastic dog that is compact enough to fit into smaller environments but with the personality of some of the most beloved breeds.

Their cuddly appearance, which lasts into adulthood, is part of the interest in these dogs. They tend to have fur that is similar in color to that of a Golden Retriever, but is curly or wavy like a Poodle's fur. Their appearance does actually have a bit more range than many other breeds because the Golden Retriever and Miniature and Toy Poodles have distinctive looks that are not at all similar. Your Miniature Goldendoodle is likely to be entirely unique, and can really stand out when you meet another Goldendoodle that is a completely different color with a different size head and limbs. Given the fact that Miniature Goldendoodles vary from small dogs to medium-sized dogs, it is understandable that their appearances are so diverse.

Miniature Goldendoodles are fairly easy to groom and are very easy to train. While there are definite differences in personality between the two parent breeds, they are known for being exceptionally companionable, sociable, energetic, and loving. Your Miniature Goldendoodle's personality can be nearly as varied as the dog's appearance, but at the core, you can expect that your dog will be loving, friendly, and a lot of fun to have around all of the time.

Because it is a designer dog, you do need to be very careful about finding the right breeder or in asking the right questions if you are adopting an older dog. You will want to learn as much about the parents' personalities as possible. For older dogs, you will want to learn about the behavior the dog has exhibited in the past so that you know what to expect. Some Miniature Goldendoodles are mellow and relaxed, and others are quite energetic and rambunctious. You will need to be prepared for the personality you are probably bringing into the family. However, they are almost always very intelligent because the parent breeds are. This means you will be able to train your new family member to better fit into your family structure once the canine arrives—just make sure you set aside the time to keep up with the training of the new family member. Miniature Goldendoodles are amazing dogs, and they are incredible companions to have around.

CHAPTER 1
A Unique Look—The Miniature Goldendoodle

The Miniature Goldendoodle is one of the most well-known designer dogs, and a large part of that is because of its larger counterpart—the Goldendoodle. As a designer dog it has a remarkably short history, and because it is not a purebred, you cannot enter it into any dog show. Given its short breeding history, the Miniature Goldendoodle, whose mother is usually a Golden Retriever and whose father is a Miniature or Toy Poodle, has gained a nearly unprecedented amount of attention.

Photo Courtesy of Sophia Georgantonis

These cute little bundles were first intentionally bred during the 1990s. They are most commonly called Miniature Goldendoodles, but they have a few other names that are also commonly used, such as Groodles and Goldiepoos. You could also call them Goldendoodles, but these varieties are smaller than the average Goldendoodle.

You will know when you see one of these cuddly bundles because they have a distinctive appearance. Between the way they look and the fact that they are considered hypoallergenic, Miniature Goldendoodles are understandably popular. They have an amazing temperament and a desire to please their people that make them easy to grow accustomed to having around all the time.

Descriptions and Defining Characteristics

One of the things that makes Miniature Goldendoodles so remarkable is that they are both adorable and intelligent because their parents are both known to be intelligent breeds. Combined with a very agreeable temperament, these pint-sized puppies can easily wriggle their way into your heart before you even realize what is going on.

Appearance

You can identify a Miniature Goldendoodle without too much trouble. Most of them have the beautiful golden color of their Golden Retriever mother, but they do come in a few other colors: cream, black, and chocolate brown. The relatively straight fur they are born with will change to either wavy or curly as the puppy ages. The fur is also very soft, and the droopy ears with curly or wavy fur around it helps add to their adorable appearance. It is difficult to refrain from reaching out and petting those soft, adorable ears.

HELPFUL TIP

No Guarantee with Hybrid Dogs

Since Miniature Goldendoodles are a cross between Toy Poodles and Golden Retrievers, instead of being a well-established breed of their own, there are no guarantees about what size your dog will be or what coat type it will have. Genetics are unpredictable, so be prepared for your puppy to grow to be larger than expected or to shed more than you think.

Their heart-shaped, black noses are the perfect accent to their adorable faces. Your Miniature Goldendoodle is likely to spend a lot of time sticking that nose into all kinds of places, particularly in your face as often as possible.

If you decide not to cut your Miniature Goldendoodle's facial hair, you will find that they quickly begin to look scruffy, which can add to their charm. Fur will grow around their eyes (which you will need to clean and brush to ensure your dog does not get dirt in his/her eyes). They will also develop what can only be called a beard, which you can change when you want to give your pup a different appearance.

Temperament

As far as their temperament goes, Miniature Goldendoodles are the result of two breeds that are beloved for being affable, intelligent, non-aggressive, and faithful. This means that it can be a real pleasure to train them because they will be happy to spend time with you and listen to you praise them when they learn new tricks. You will not only enjoy the time spent together, but you will also be able to show off just how clever your dog is when you have people to visit (or while you are out walking). While they can be persuaded by food, for the most part the Miniature Goldendoodle is incredibly loyal. You don't have to worry about them being aggressive, but they are very good at letting you know when there is something wrong. Their protective nature means they can work as decent guard dogs, but mostly as alarms rather than protection.

You can also rest easy about introducing them to your current pets because Miniature Goldendoodles tend to love everyone and everything as long as they don't pose a risk to the dog's people.

They actually have a fairly large size variation depending on the size of the father (whether the sire is a Miniature or Toy Poodle). You can expect your Miniature Goldendoodle to be between 13 and 20 inches long and weigh from 15 to 35 pounds. This does mean that your dog could be classified as either a small or medium-sized dog, which isn't common for a breed. If you plan to adopt a puppy, make sure to ask about the parents' breeds so that you have a rough idea of how large your dog will be when it is fully grown.

Defining the Golden Retriever Characteristics

Golden Retrievers are a breed that has consistently remained one of the most popular family dogs, as well as being a great work dog. Along with the Labrador Retriever, the Golden Retriever has always retained a high level of popularity even as other breeds are adopted due to fads, and then fade away. This has a lot to do with their appearance and their temperament. They are a medium-sized dog with a fair level of energy, but long daily walks make them good in any environment. Beautiful, intelligent, and friendly—it is obvious why these dogs are so beloved.

Appearance

You have probably encountered them on walks—they are impossible to miss. Golden Retrievers are one of the first breeds that people think of when they hear the word "dog," and that is because they have always remained popular. The idea of a "dog" has largely been shaped by people's constant inclusion of them in families (Labradors and Beagles are the other dogs commonly imagined because of how common the breeds are). They have long legs with a sleek body, but the first thing you probably notice is the long, golden coat. They got their name from this lovely and soft fur coat that lends an elegant touch to their large, slender bodies.

They have been work dogs for a very long time, so they are also quite muscular. Their fur is thick and fairly long. Their heads are broad, but their large, dark eyes really stand out against the beautiful fur. With a long, slender nose (that they love to put in your face for kisses) and short, soft, floppy ears, their faces are easy for anyone to adore.

Golden Retrievers have a sleek, medium build, giving them an elegant gait that really shows off their luxurious hair as it sways during a walk. Their legs are long for their bodies, and they have robust chest areas, which helps them run further, faster.

In addition to being a stunning-looking dog, the Golden Retriever has a winning personality. They love adventures, staying at home, meeting new people, working, resting, training, playing, and goofing off. Perhaps best known for being one of the most affable breeds, they are not aggressive. Gentle with both children and small animals, Golden Retrievers make great family pets.

Temperament

Photo Courtesy of Ashley Stella

As an incredibly intelligent breed, their even temperament makes them ideal for working as support dogs. Golden Retrievers are often employed as seeing eye dogs, emotional support dogs, and other types of assistance work.

They are incredibly fun-loving and playful when they aren't working. This can include learning tricks that will make you laugh and help you bond with your dog. You can take them out hiking and romping around in the yard. This makes them the perfect companions for regular activities and for vacationing in new places.

While they may not be aggressive, they are terribly protective of their people. If a Golden Retriever has its hackles up, that is all the warning you need to know that there is something wrong. They will typically stand between you and any perceived danger because their first priority is to protect their pack.

Defining the Toy and Miniature Poodle Characteristics

Miniature and Toy Poodles are almost exactly like the Standard Poodle, except that they are much smaller. They are what make the Miniature Goldendoodle small since they are the diminutive versions of the Standard Poodle. Their size is one of their most defining characteristics because it gives people in apartments and small homes the ability to have an amazing dog that easily fits into a small environment. Miniature and Toy Poodles have an even temperament and a loving disposition just like their larger counterpart. There are many reasons why Miniature and Toy Poodles are a popular alternative to the large Standard Poodle.

Appearance

Photo Courtesy of
Joyce Hughes

Both are younger breeds than the Standard Poodle, but the Miniature and Toy Poodles have been around for several centuries. With the popularity and gentle nature of the Poodle, wealthy people wanted their own Poodle companion, but such a large dog was more difficult to have as a constant companion. Toy and Miniature Poodles are dogs that were bred specifically to be lap dogs for members of the nobility, like many other smaller dogs.

Apart from their small stature, everything else about the Miniature and Toy Poodles' appearance makes them easily identifiable as being part of the Poodle family. They have very curly fur that can look scruffy when not cut. You can have them groomed to look very stylish, including the classic Poodle cut with the fur cut to look like puff balls on their legs and head. Everything is proportionally sized down from the long elegant legs of a Standard Poodle to the nose.

Temperament

Photo Courtesy of Lisa Snyder

Beyond being easy to groom to look fashionable, Poodles have been loved for centuries because of how affable and intelligent they are. The smaller versions have the same confidence and dignity of a Standard Poodle, but also some of the energy and exuberance associated with small dogs. Size is never a hindrance to them as they bounce around the home trying to get people to play with them. They tend to stay near people because they have been people's companions for centuries. They want to be with their people, no exceptions.

You do have to be careful with both versions of the small Poodles because it is easy to treat them too leniently, which can result in many of the problems associated with small dogs. In addition to developing small dog syndrome, Miniature and Toy Poodles may suffer from anxiety, particularly separation anxiety. As long as you make sure to train them (keeping a consistent and firm approach), they can be incredibly loving, though you are going to have to work on making sure they do not feel anxious.

CHAPTER 2
Breed History and Characteristics

The Miniature Goldendoodle is a relatively new dog breed (particularly compared to the extensive history of the two parent breeds) that is likely to continue being bred for a long time. These pups take some of the best characteristics from both breeds to make a great companion, even for those people who have allergies. The majority of Miniature Goldendoodles are first generation (meaning both of their parents are different breeds, and not Miniature Goldendoodles). This does mean that the personality of your dog will be uncertain until the canine reaches adulthood.

However, since the parents have fairly similar personalities, the core aspects of your designer dog are pretty predictable. This is why the young breed has become so immensely popular in such a short time.

Photo Courtesy of
Patti Fousch

A Short History

Goldendoodles of all sizes have the same history because breeders knew that people would desire different sizes based on their current homes and environments. However, the first few Goldendoodles were a cross breed between a Standard Poodle and a Golden Retriever. The first pairs of parents were known, but the date and year are not; it is known that it was in the 1990s, and breeders began marketing them by the end of the 1990s.

The breed was likely inspired by the Labradoodle, which became popular because it allowed those who have allergies to have a friendly Lab-like dog with minimal shedding and little to no dander. With Golden Retrievers being as popular as Labrador Retrievers, it was logical to breed them with Poodles too. The Goldendoodle has proven to be as popular as the Labradoodle, and soon people were wanting them in different sizes.

for people to intentionally create a new breed because many older breeds have the same traits through normal selective breeding. It is easier to predict the potential risks and problems with a single breed than by trying to get a consistent new breed through two different breeds.

Photo Courtesy of Liza Rieke

The American Kennel Club's concerns are certainly legitimate, particularly because of puppy mills that seek to quickly profit from designer dog trends. Before selecting a breeder, take the time to do your research. You want to find a breeder who knows the parents well and takes very good care of them. You also want to find a breeder who can tell you about the parents, their personalities, and their parentage. For designer dogs, you want to find breeders who love dogs and know how to breed them right, and not people who are simply trying to make a lot of money off of the trend.

Unpredictable Traits

The American Kennel Club's assertion that designer dogs' traits are more difficult to predict is very true, even for a breed as adorable as the Miniature Goldendoodle. There are many similarities between Golden Retriever and Poodle personalities, but there are enough differences that it is difficult to know what to look for in terms of health problems or personality traits of the puppies.

Overlapping traits between the two breeds do make it easy to figure out the basic personality. The size of your Miniature Goldendoodle will be unpredictable because there is a significant difference in size between Golden Retrievers and Miniature or Toy Poodles. Whatever their size, they will be incredibly loving because both of the parent breeds love people, particularly their family members.

Golden Retrievers are employed as therapy, guide, and help dogs for a reason. They have an incredibly patient, gentle temperament that means they can put up with a lot without it being obvious. This breed is mellow, calm, and generally quiet. If your dog takes after the Golden Retriever, you can expect your Miniature Goldendoodle to be very easygoing.

HELPFUL TIP
A Short History Means Less Predictability

Even though Labradoodles and Goldendoodles first appeared around 20 years ago, Miniature Goldendoodles have only become popular within the last 5-10 years. Not only does that mean that many Miniature Goldendoodles are first or second generation, but few Miniature Goldendoodles have reached old age, meaning there's no way to know for sure how long they'll live or what health problems they may deal with as they age.

Miniature Poodles are very friendly, bouncy, and energetic. They can also be a bit of a handful if not properly trained. Of course, they are incredibly loving, but your Miniature Goldendoodle may be a lot more energetic and bouncy if it takes after the father.

Either way, both personalities will make the dog incredibly loving and fun to be around as they age.

CHAPTER 3
The Ideal Home

The Miniature Goldendoodle looks like a cuddly little ball of fluff that doesn't shed like a Golden Retriever does. Because of their small size, they can fit into any environment comfortably, including small and studio apartments. They are also a fairly quiet dog, so you won't have to worry about your Miniature Goldendoodle barking at all of the noises around you, which is great when you live in an apartment. They are loving, have moderate energy levels, and are incredibly friendly, which makes them an ideal family dog. Naturally, there are some environments where they fare better than others, but as long as you make time to walk and play with them, they should be all right even if there is no yard or fenced-in area available.

Photo Courtesy of
Denise Peek

The Miniature Goldendoodle can be a pretty energetic dog, but you may also get a dog that is pretty mellow. Either way, your Miniature Goldendoodle will have ample energy to play and experience adventures together with you. Since this breed doesn't usually get bigger than 30 pounds, it is easy to address their exercise needs. For an intelligent dog, they don't tend to be destructive. Any bad habits they develop, like gnawing on furniture or stealing your clothes, you should be able train out of them fairly easily. Making sure that they get adequate exercise will also curb those unwanted behaviors.

Best Environment

There are many reasons why people have fallen in love with the Miniature Goldendoodle. They are affable, cuddly, intelligent, and fun to have around. Since this breed is usually easy to train, you have a lot of options for entertainment—they love to be the center of attention, and if you are laughing, they love that even more. Once they are trained, they are nearly a perfect dog, and can fit into almost any environment. However, there are some places that are better for them than others.

A Compact Canine For Any Home

The Miniature Goldendoodle is a wonderful companion, and given their small stature, they tend to do well in nearly any environment. Pretty much wherever you are, your dog is going to be there with you. If you are home, they are going to be like an adorable shadow that accompanies you into every room in the house, so you aren't likely to get any time alone once your pup comes home with you.

They are a great first dog because they tend to love everybody, making them perfect for a family with kids. Larger families are also great for this breed of dog because then they aren't left alone very often. Be prepared for your Miniature Goldendoodle to be very clingy, and it will likely suffer from separation anxiety. If you can work from home or will have someone in your home most of the time, that will be the best option for your pup. If you have other dogs in your home, that will also be best for your little canine. However, if you tend to work long days and there are no other people or dogs at home, this is not the best environment for a Miniature Goldendoodle. The long hours alone can have a very negative effect on this dog breed.

Just because you have a Miniature Goldendoodle doesn't mean that you can't leave your dog alone occasionally. They can be by themselves (although if you have more than one dog, that is better for them) for a few hours at a time. If you have trained them, you won't need to worry about them getting into much trouble most of the time. However, you may want to make sure that trashcans are inaccessible.

If you need a therapy dog, this is a nearly perfect breed. You will probably have your dog by your side almost all of the time. Because of their intelligence, they will be able to quickly adjust to your needs and will happily help you when you need it most. Since they are also very sociable, they will be great when the two of you are out in public, and they will keep their focus on you.

Even No Yard Is Fine—As Long As Your Miniature Goldendoodle Gets Moderate Exercise

Photo Courtesy of Jessica Fitzgerald

Always remember that the Golden Retriever is a work dog. Even if the Poodle side is dominant, your dog is going to have a lot of energy and a desire to be doing more than just sitting around. Since it is a smaller dog, it won't need to be as active as a Golden Retriever because its short legs mean that walking will use more energy to go the same distance as a Golden Retriever. As long as you ensure that your canine gets daily exercise, your canine should be fine. Typically, a solid 30 minutes of exercise should be good, especially when combined with some supplemental training and short walks. Daily play will be incredibly entertaining, and will make the exercise feel much less like work.

If you can't walk for 30 minutes a day, you should have a yard or some place that you can go so that your dog can get the necessary exercise. You can hang out in the backyard throwing a ball or other toy and your dog will be perfectly happy running and retrieving it. This is a great exercise that you can easily work into your average day. A trained Miniature Goldendoodle means that you can find a lot of other amusing games to play that will tire your dog. You can also take your dog to a dog park to run out their energy and provide a large portion of the exercise they require for the day.

Fantastic, Intelligent Companion

The Miniature Goldendoodle is a breed that is a lot of fun to have around because they adore attention and fun. They aren't known for being a vocal breed either, which can be very nice if you live in an apartment. If your dog barks, it is probable that there is a good reason for it. Since they aren't large, they aren't great guard dogs, even if they tend to want to protect you. However, they can let you know when there is potential danger nearby, and they will be more than willing to help protect you in any way they can.

Training is incredibly important because they need to be mentally stimulated. It is very easy to do though. These dogs enjoy being with people and can understand human emotions as well as another human (if not more than many humans). If you are having fun training, your dog will enjoy it too. It is also good physical exercise because they can be very agile. You will quickly realize that they are able to understand new commands remarkably fast—this makes training very rewarding to both of you. Spend some time looking through the kinds of tricks you want to teach your dog, and once they have the basics down, you will be able to move on to the more entertaining commands.

*Photo Courtesy of
Janice Dockum*

Floor Surfaces

Smooth surfaces can be challenging for these pups. While the breed is small, it does not mean that they have better traction, just that they are closer to the ground when they fall. If they get excited and start running around, they could get hurt on a floor with a smoother surface. Hardwood, tile, and vinyl can be tricky for any canine. Any amusement you find in watching your dog lose their footing is vastly outweighed by the potential danger and harm if they fall and get hurt or slam into the wall or furniture because they cannot stop.

Putting carpeting or adding non-skid throw rugs in these areas can make them safer for your Miniature Goldendoodle.

Nearly Perfect Family Pet

This designer dog is easily one of the most perfect dogs for a family. Their adoration for people, including kids, is pretty well known. Even if you adopt an older dog, as long as you introduce them to your family in a quiet environment they are likely to acclimate quickly to their new home. As a canine that loves to be surrounded by people, they love nearly everyone they meet. They tend to be patient with kids, although you will need to spend time preparing your young children and always monitor their interactions with your new family member. Once the kids learn how to interact with your new dog, this breed can be an ideal companion for any age person. You will want to make sure your children know to be careful with your dog because you don't want the kids to accidentally hurt the dog.

Ideal Lifestyle

The most defining personality trait of the majority of Miniature Goldendoodles is how sociable and fun-loving they are, especially with their family members. It is incredibly easy to bond with this breed because they are happiest when you are spending time with them. It is likely they will want to sit with you on the furniture and in your bed. If you don't want dogs on the bed, you are going to have to start training for that early and always be consistent—if you let your dog on the couch or bed once, it is going to be very difficult to teach them that it is not allowed.

You will need to ensure they get adequate exercise, and that they are not overeating. The right balance will help keep them healthy and happy.

*Photo Courtesy of
Nicole Chapple*

Strengths

Since the Miniature Goldendoodle is an extremely social breed, it is easy to feel like your canine understands you and your emotions. They are very attentive and affectionate, reacting to how you are feeling without you having to say anything, and they make it clear that you are an important part of their world. This desire to be with you and have fun is why this intelligent dog isn't headstrong or difficult to train from the beginning. Positive reinforcement, especially praise and petting, is more than enough to encourage them to keep training. If you train your Miniature Goldendoodle, you aren't likely to have much trouble with them.

Common Exercise Benefits

When you aren't playing with them, Miniature Goldendoodles are more than happy to just cuddle with you as you watch TV or work on your computer. It may take a while to tire them out since they have a good bit of energy, but because of their small size a brisk walk can help expend that energy. This makes them less than ideal as a jogging partner if they are on the smaller end of the breed size. If you are a slow jogger, you will still need to keep the distance you run a little shorter because your dog will likely be unable to keep up with you for longer jogs. Once you finish a jog, you can plop down and play with your dog as you relax. Activities like fetch and tug of war are more than enough to keep them happy while you rest.

If you want to increase your daily walking steps, your dog is a great addition to your family and routine. You and your spouse (or your entire family) can make the most of your new family member while going out on walks. The dog will love the time spent exploring while getting to know the family, and you will have an excuse to talk with those you love without overexerting yourself.

Pleasers—Plan To Train Them

Training is incredibly important for your Miniature Goldendoodle, and you will need to be consistent in your training. You won't need to be firm or establish an alpha position because your dog is going to want to have fun with you and will be willing to do what you say as long as you give them attention. But if you aren't consistent with your training and applying the rules, you will have trouble because your dog is going to learn when it can break the rules.

Training the Miniature Goldendoodle is relatively easy because they really love positive reinforcement. Given their small stature, this is a great piece of news because you don't want to use treats as an incentive too often. Praise and playtime are some of the best ways of getting your dog to learn a wide range of tricks and behaviors. If you don't train your dog, they may suffer from the same kinds of undesirable behaviors as other small dogs because you haven't discouraged them from acting that way. Since they are so easy to train, it is well worth the time, and you will probably start seeing results a lot sooner than with other breeds, even some of the more intelligent dogs.

Remember that you shouldn't be leaving them home alone for long periods of time because they may feel separation anxiety. Being quick learners will not diminish the anxiety. Having another dog as a constant companion can help minimize this, and your Miniature Goldendoodle may be a good influence on your other dog during training.

Hypoallergenic

CAUTION
Hypoallergenic?

Despite claims that Miniature Goldendoodles are hypoallergenic, no dog is truly hypoallergenic. That's because people are allergic to a dog's dander and saliva, not its fur. Fur that doesn't shed keeps more dander on the dog, and thus, less is left around the home environment, meaning dogs that don't shed tend to bother people's allergies less. However, they still aren't truly hypoallergenic. It's also important to remember that since Miniature Goldendoodles are part Golden Retriever, they can still shed.

In addition to being incredibly loving dogs, Miniature Goldendoodles are popular because they are considered hypoallergenic. However, this can vary based on the parents. Many of them shed very little and even people who suffer from allergies are likely to find that they can interact with their Miniature Goldendoodle without medication or constant sneezing. This designer dog's coat is incredibly easy to maintain and that makes them a fantastic addition to any home. They won't be covering your furniture and all of the corners of your home with dog hair either (something that Golden Retrievers are known for doing), which means that you are not going to see a significant rise in cleaning your home once your new family member arrives.

This doesn't mean you are completely off the hook for cleaning and brushing though. You just aren't going to need to spend time every single day keeping the shedding to a minimum the way you would with a Golden Retriever. Regular brushing is required to keep your Miniature Goldendoodle from getting matted hair, but you won't have to worry about having as much dog hair around your home.

A Little Dog For Those Who Love Cuddling And Playing

The Miniature Goldendoodle is bred to be a loving, cuddly dog that can make anyone feel better. They want to spend all of their time with you, playing and sleeping. When you want to go outside, they are game for it. If it is raining and you just want to sit around, that is fine with them too. They are the perfect friend because what they really want is to be with you. That means whatever you want to do is perfectly fine with them.

Photo Courtesy of
Sonja Burns

Do be prepared for them to want to constantly be with you. Being alone is pretty much a thing of the past once a Miniature Goldendoodle is in your home, but with the right training, that can be perfect.

When you have company, they will be just as excited to welcome your company as you are. Typically, you won't have to worry about them becoming aggressive with anyone (although you do need to make sure young children aren't too rough with them). Any dogs already in your home will be just as exciting and enjoyable to your Miniature Golden-doodle as the people in your home. This is the kind of dog that is just full of love and attention, and really all they ask is that you be there with them. It is the reason that they are so popular and lovable.

CHAPTER 4
Finding Your Miniature Goldendoodle

If you have reached this point in the book, you are probably ready to dive into getting your own adorable bundle. This chapter will help you determine whether to choose a puppy or an older dog. If you are up for all of the work that comes with training a puppy, this chapter will help you find the right breeder.

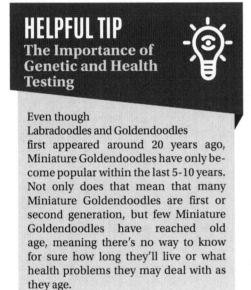

HELPFUL TIP

The Importance of Genetic and Health Testing

Even though Labradoodles and Goldendoodles first appeared around 20 years ago, Miniature Goldendoodles have only become popular within the last 5-10 years. Not only does that mean that many Miniature Goldendoodles are first or second generation, but few Miniature Goldendoodles have reached old age, meaning there's no way to know for sure how long they'll live or what health problems they may deal with as they age.

The Miniature Goldendoodle is a breed that is great for playing with inside the house or out in nature, as well as being fantastic for cuddling with during the long, dark days of winter. They are one of the easiest dog breeds to incorporate into any family. This means that the kinds of adventures and memories that you will make together are nearly endless. For the best fit, you will want to pay attention to the basics and ask the right questions during the adoption process.

Every Miniature Goldendoodle is different, but this designer dog does have some predictable personality traits. Typically, they aren't destructive despite being intelligent. They have a moderate amount of energy, so they aren't likely to be too energetic once they outgrow the puppy phase. Mostly, they want to be with their people, getting your attention and making sure you are content.

However, you will need to be mindful of the fact that the Miniature Goldendoodle is a designer dog when you start the process. Puppy mills are all too common with designer breeds, and you need to be able to watch for the signs so that you can avoid them. You also need to understand that the breeder should not be a part of a puppy mill if you want to ensure that your puppy is healthy. Since this is not one of the older established breeds, your dog's health will be less certain. The puppy could take on health problems from either of the parent breeds.

Adopting From A Breeder

If you want to adopt a Miniature Goldendoodle puppy, there are a number of considerations you need to work through prior to selecting your puppy. You want a happy, healthy puppy, and that is harder with designer puppies because puppy mills try to cash in on the popularity of a particular breed. They do not give any consideration to the health or needs of their puppies. You will need to find a reputable breeder, which is the first step in the process to adopting your newest family member.

Photo Courtesy of Sonja Burns

Finding A Breeder

With a breed as popular as the Miniature Goldendoodle, you are going to have a lot of breeders to research. Finding a responsible breeder is the best thing you can do for your puppy since good breeders work with only healthy parents, reducing the odds that a puppy will have serious health issues. There aren't too many certified breeders because of how new the breed is. Coupled with the booming popularity, puppy mills and less capable breeders are looking to make money quickly from that popularity. It is the reason you need to be particularly careful and plan to spend a lot of time researching before deciding on your puppy.

Start by looking for certified breeders. Find out the adoption timeline and decide if it is right for your family. Be prepared for it to be more than a year because certified breeders typically have lists and make sure to take care of the parents and puppies. This means giving the mothers adequate time between pregnancies to recover and live a life. If you find that the timeline is too long, you may turn to non-certified breeders, but you will also need to plan to spend more time asking questions to ensure the parents and puppies are treated well and that health issues are taken into account before breeding. The following is a list of questions you should ask to understand the parents' history. Be prepared for each call to last at least an hour. If the breeder is unwilling to dedicate enough time to answer your questions, cross them off of your list of breeders—all good breeders are willing to make time to talk about the parents and the dogs.

① → ● Can you visit the property to take a look at the parents? If the immediate answer is no, then do not bother to continue. Even if you do not intend to go to the location, the breeders should be willing to let potential puppy parents check out the parents of the puppy. The only exception is if the breeders keep regular blogs and camera footage that you can review. You need to be able to see the conditions and environment that the puppies live in, and you want to see the parents to make sure they are treated well.

② → ● Ask about health tests and certifications for the parents. Breeders need to have all of the tests and certifications for the parents to ensure that you receive the healthiest puppy possible. Good breeders will often have guarantees against the worst genetic issues. If the breeder is not offering this guarantee, do not continue.

3 → ● Breeders should take care of all of the basics for the puppies, such as the initial vaccines and wormings. It is essential for puppies to have these medical procedures taken care of when they are six weeks old (too early for them to leave their mother), and you will be responsible for continuing them. After the shots and wormings are started, they need to be continued every three weeks afterward, which means they will be well into receiving their shots before the puppy comes to your home.

● Find out how the breeder takes care of the puppies during the earliest stage of their lives. This will help you know how much work you have to do as well. You will want to keep a consistent training program with the dog, and that will be much easier if you continue the training the breeder started. The breeder may also have begun different types of training, such as house and crate training. You will need to know that information before getting your puppy home.

● Ask for their advice on raising your puppy. A good breeder can make recommendations and will give you options on how to handle some of the less enjoyable phases, as well as the things that your puppy is likely to love. A great breeder will also be there to answer questions about your Miniature Goldendoodle long after your dog has reached maturity. They are interested in the dog's well-being and are willing to answer questions over the canine's entire life span.

● Ask if they breed F1 Miniature Goldendoodles, or the first generation of the breed. This means that the breeder only works with one parent who is a Golden Retriever and one parent who is a Miniature Poodle. They do not breed with Miniature Goldendoodles, only with the two original breeds.

● Get details about the parents, such as their age, weight, size, how many litters they have had, how many puppies they usually have in a litter, and their health. See if you can get current pictures of the parents and their previous puppies, to help you know generally what your puppy will look like.

Health Tests And Certifications

The best place to start is by reviewing the Goldendoodle Association of North America website . The site provides details on the minimum requirements that breeders must meet to gain membership status. Their site shows the different levels of membership and what tests are required for a breeder to qualify for that level. The higher the breeder's membership level, the more tests they have conducted to ensure the puppies will be as healthy as possible. However, this is not a standard used by all associations.

You should check the heath tests and certifications of the parents.

- Golden Retrievers should be tested for hip dysplasia, elbow dysplasia, eye disease, and heart disease.
- Miniature Poodles should be tested for hip dysplasia, eye disease, Progressive Retinal Atrophy, and Patellar Luxation.

*Photo Courtesy of
Sunflower Farms Mini GoldenDoodles*

Photo Courtesy of Kelly Sayers

Contracts And Guarantees

Even though they are designer dogs, you want to find a breeder who offers a guarantee for the puppies. This demonstrates the breeder's confidence that the parents are not passing hereditary conditions on to the puppies, providing greater odds that your puppy will have a better quality of life.

Contracts and guarantees come with information on the health of the puppy and recommendations for you, the new puppy parent, to follow on how best to raise the puppy. The breeder may strongly recommend that you visit a vet within a couple of days of the puppy coming home to get a baseline for the puppy's health. During this visit, the vet will test the puppy for possible issues so that you can act on any early signs or symptoms, minimizing or eliminating those issues so that the puppy grows up to be healthy. In the event that a major issue or ailment is detected, a guarantee allows you to return the puppy to the breeder, and you will be able to select a new puppy. This ensures you receive a healthy puppy.

Puppy Genetics—The Parents

Designer breeds can be a challenge to own because of the unpredictable combination of potential ailments that puppies can inherit. Instead of being able to look at possible issues that Golden Retrievers may suffer, you have to be mindful of the genetic problems of both Golden Retrievers and Miniature Poodles. However, since the puppy is not a purebred dog, the mixed heritage could mean fewer health risks. If both parents are healthy and come from healthy lines, the puppies are less likely to have problems because of their genetics.

The temperament and personality of the parents also determine the same characteristics for the puppies. While the core of both of the breeds' temperaments are the same, their personalities can be fairly different. A puppy that takes after a Golden Retriever is much more likely to be mellow and easy to train. A puppy that takes after the Miniature Poodle is likely to be more active and friskier. Socialization should be fairly easy, but training a mellow puppy and training an energetic puppy are very different.

Selecting Your Puppy

Selecting a puppy is the same, regardless of breed. You want to look for the puppy that displays a personality that you think will fit best with your family. Unlike many breeds, your Miniature Goldendoodle's core traits will be fairly predictable, so you will be looking at traits like energy level and friskiness. You will need to see the puppies either in person or in a video.

Photo Courtesy of Stefanie Stevens

Watch how the puppies interact with each other. The ones that interact more can indicate how well the puppy will interact with your current pets, as well as showing off their personalities.

Watch the overall interaction of all the puppies as well. If it seems like the majority of them are more hyperactive or aggressive, then you may want to wait for another litter. This is typically not a problem with this breed, but it is an example of the kind of group behavior to watch for. Similarly, you want to avoid litters where the puppies seem generally scared and skittish. You will want to make sure the puppies have healthy interactions to ensure that your puppy is not likely to exhibit behaviors that will make training more difficult or socializing a challenge.

Then pay attention to the individual puppies to determine which one you think will work best with your family. The puppies that are very outgoing may be more demanding of attention in the home, while the ones who hang back could be lower maintenance. If all of the puppies pile forward to meet you (which is nearly a guarantee with Miniature Goldendoodle litters), figure out which one you feel you could bond with the fastest.

When you are picking the puppy, look for the one that exhibits the desired personality traits you want. If you want a forward, friendly, excitable dog, the first one to greet you may be the one you seek. If you want a dog that will think things through and let others get more attention, this is a mellower dog that may be better for your home.

Beware Of Puppy Mills

With all designer dogs, you have to be very wary of puppy mills. The dog parents in these mills are treated poorly and health issues (both current and genetic) are likely to be ignored by the breeders. This could cause significant problems for the puppies as potential health issues will be ignored in them as well. Puppy mills don't tend to offer contracts or guarantees, and the puppies probably will not have had all of the necessary medical attention prior to leaving the parents.

Puppy mills have earned their bad reputation, and many of them are shut down for having poor living conditions for their dogs and puppies. They are only interested in breeding for a quick profit, and will do only the minimum to care for the puppies. When puppy mills are shut down, the dogs and puppies end up with rescue organizations. You can get your puppy from a rescuer, but there is a higher risk of genetic problems.

Adopting An Older Dog

With as much time and energy as you need to put into puppies, an older Miniature Goldendoodle is the right dog for some families. Since they are a newer breed, it is harder to find a rescue association, but that doesn't mean that the rescue groups aren't out there.

Benefits

If you don't want to spend a lot of time on basic training, you definitely do not want to bring a puppy into your home—not even a Miniature Goldendoodle. They are easier to train than many other dogs, but puppies can still cause a mess and require a lot more time than an adult dog. Puppies will cause you to lose sleep and to have to clean up accidents in the house, which means you will need a lot of patience. If you select an adult, you can skip right into the more enjoyable training and bonding. This is really the appeal of an adult Miniature Goldendoodle.

Already housebroken and able to quickly pick up on training, this breed is fantastic to bring into the home as an adult. They are likely to bond with your family relatively quickly because they adore being with people. Learning your habits and preferences will be something they can enjoy for a while, and then they will just enjoy staying close and doing things with you and your family. They have a great attention span and can pick up on human facial cues a lot faster than many other breeds. As they reach their golden years, they will become couch potatoes, as long as they get at least 30 minutes of walking.

Adult Miniature Goldendoodles are definitely a great fit for individuals who don't want to train a dog or who have busy families (as long as there is going to be people or dogs around to keep them company so the Miniature Goldendoodle doesn't suffer from separation anxiety). You will need to be prepared to monitor adult dogs if you already have pets, especially if you don't know how or if they were socialized. You will need to be present to ensure there is no tension between your new family member and your existing furry companions.

Rescues

Designer dogs, including Miniature Goldendoodles, don't have many dedicated rescue operations available to set up an adoption. A large portion of the Miniature Goldendoodles currently in shelters and rescue systems are there because of the shutdown of puppy mills with poor breeding practices and unhealthy environmental conditions. This does not mean that there is definitely something wrong with the dog, but you will want to monitor your new dog more closely, and you should plan for additional testing in the first few months.

You can look around your area for local rescues that specialize in the breed. Make sure to set aside time to visit the rescue facility to check out the conditions the dogs are living in before you choose a dog. You should also ask about references or read reviews online to see what kinds of experiences you are likely to have with the rescue group. This is equally true if you go to a shelter.

Most shelters and rescue organizations will establish requirements for your dog because they want to find the right forever home for their dogs. Once a dog leaves, they want to make sure that the dog is treated well and does not end up back at the shelter needing a new home. You are not likely to have any information on the health and personality of the parents, which means vet visits are going to be critical for your Miniature Goldendoodle. Shelters and rescue groups do some of this, but typically cannot complete a full battery of tests that can help you identify any potential health issues. This means you are going to need to plan to spend a bit more money to ensure the health of your dog, but you aren't going to need to keep returning to the vet like you would with a puppy.

Introduction To Children And Other Pets

Adult Miniature Goldendoodles are already trained to a certain point, and you can retrain them to stop behaviors you don't like. However, if they were not socialized when they were young, they may not be as patient with children and other pets. You will want to know the adult Miniature Goldendoodle's history with small animals and children before adopting them. If there is no certainty that the dog has been exposed to either children or other animals, you will need to be extra careful about the introductions once you get home.

Miniature Goldendoodle aren't aggressive or territorial, but children and other pets can be a unique challenge for any dog that has never lived with them. Make sure your child understands that there will be no playing with the dog without adult supervision for the first week, at the very least. You probably will want to keep play supervised for the first month to make sure your dog is adjusting well to the new environment. Your Miniature Goldendoodle will be more accepting of the children and other pets once the dog feels safer. They are people pleasers, but you want to make sure there is no unnecessary stress on them while they are getting familiar with their new environment.

CHAPTER 5
Preparing For Your Puppy

Preparing for your Miniature Goldendoodle is going to be every bit as time consuming and critical as it is to prepare for an infant in your home. Before you give way to all of the excitement that comes with bringing a cutie home, you need to spend a considerable amount of time looking over your home and making sure everything is safe for your newest family member. You can begin when you start looking for the right breeder, or you can wait until closer to arrival time; however, make sure that you are preparing for your puppy for at least a week before the arrival (although two weeks to a month is better to make sure you don't miss anything). The preparation will keep you occupied so that time goes a little faster, and you will feel as though you have your puppy that much quicker.

Photo Courtesy of Denise Peek

Preparing Your Kids

Kids are the best starting point because they are going to be just as excited as you are. The younger they are, the earlier you are going to need to start helping them prepare. Even though they can be a hardy dog with a fantastic temperament, you want your kids to be careful with the Miniature Goldendoodle puppy. This will mean that everyone has fun.

Since your kids are probably going to spend more time with your new dog than you are, you need to ensure that they know how to behave with a little puppy. As soon as your Miniature Goldendoodle puppy arrives, your kids are going to be too excited to try to learn anything new. That means they have to already know the best way to interact with the family's new addition.

Establish rules, and frequently ask your kids about different scenarios to ensure they know what they should do. With the arrival of your Miniature Goldendoodle, your kids will know the rules and you can monitor that the kids abide by those rules. If your children are too excited, it will be easier to remind them of the rules through questions than if you haven't been over the rules a number of times prior to the puppy's arrival. With gentle reminders, your kids can modify how they play with the puppy, and you will be able to let them play a little longer. This benefits you the most because the puppy and kids will be able to tire each other out, and you will have a little more time to relax.

Do not leave your Miniature Goldendoodle alone with the children for the first few days to make sure they don't get too excited or rough while playing together, especially if you bring home a puppy that hasn't learned how to express happiness or pain. Miniature Goldendoodles still have that puppy need to teethe, and you don't want them learning to do that on anyone's arms. If your kids play too roughly, the little canine will learn bad habits that will be difficult to correct later.

The following are five rules you should start teaching your children as soon as you begin searching for a breeder. It will help them build a better bond from the beginning.

1. Be gentle. As adorable as they are, Miniature Goldendoodle puppies are small and are not up for rough play. It is never a good idea to be rough with a puppy, or even an adult Miniature Goldendoodle.

   Make sure your children understand the consequences if they play too rough with the new family member. Nipping is a common puppy or dog tendency when they feel threatened, so it is important to make sure the kids don't scare the dog. To avoid drama, teach your child that rough play is not good for the dog.

2. Chase is an outdoor game only. This will be difficult for children to remember because it is so tempting to start running with a Miniature Goldendoodle. They are so cute as their little eyes light up while they try to run to catch up, but you do not want your children or dog running through your home. Not only is your puppy (or child) likely to get hurt running in the home, it can create a feeling of insecurity for the Miniature Goldendoodle. Even if your little friend feels safe, you don't want the dog running around as an adult—once that behavior is learned, it is difficult to train your dog not to run in the home.

3. Avoid mixing mealtime and playtime. They may have an easy temperament, but all dogs have a need to protect their food from others. Your Miniature Goldendoodle should be left alone to eat in peace instead of feeling like the food might be stolen from him. It is also good for your children to focus on eating their meals as you do not want them feeding your puppy from their plates. Miniature Goldendoodles are not typically aggressive, but you don't want your puppy to learn to be anxious at mealtime.

4. The puppy should be left on its own feet—it shouldn't be picked up. Young children in particular need to be reminded that puppies are not stuffed animals—they are not there to be constantly picked up and carried around. Even if your child is careful, it can be incredibly uncomfortable for the Miniature Goldendoodle puppy to be lifted up off the floor. The puppy may be small, but children often cannot provide adequate support for a puppy's back half. This can end up hurting the puppy, particularly the spine. Even older children should not be picking up the puppy because if the puppy nips at them, the surprising pain could result in dropping the puppy.

The great thing about Miniature Goldendoodles is that there are plenty of games that can be played right there on the floor, and they will be fairly coordinated early in their lives. All they want is to play, giving kids an excuse to crawl on the floor and see what kinds of games are the most fun. This is just as true outside as inside the house as your dog will love to romp in the yard or park. You will need to make sure to follow your own rules—if you are picking up the puppy, your kids will definitely do the same.

5. Anything that is valuable needs to be kept out of reach of both your puppy and your child. Kids don't tend to be very discerning when it comes to playing, and they are likely to just grab whatever is within reach to play with the puppy. To keep mementos and valuables safe, be proactive and put valuable things out of reach. It isn't just children either—teenagers are not any more likely to pay attention when there is a little bundle of fur in front of them. Stuffed animals, towels, and anything that you don't want torn up or dirtied should be out of the areas where any playing occurs.

Preparing Your Current Dogs

Preparing your dog or dogs for a new puppy can be a unique challenge, depending on the breed or breeds you have. Even if you have introduced your dogs to other canines, it is different when you bring a new dog into your home permanently. You will need to prepare your dogs, and that is going to be considerably different than preparing your children. There is no pre-puppy conversation or rules for them to learn. Instead, you will be preparing their spaces so that they feel less threatened about having a puppy in their home. Here are several tasks you can finish before your puppy arrives.

Establish an area just for the puppy. Don't leave your puppy alone with your other dog or dogs—there should always be an adult around when the puppy and other pets are interacting. Even if you work at home, you should only let them play together if you can give them your full attention. If you can't, the puppy should not be left alone with kids or dogs. Instead, place the little canine in the designated puppy area until you or another adult can monitor the interactions.

The designated puppy area should not include anything that belongs to your other dogs, nor should the puppy's area include a location that is one of your current dog's favorite places. If your dog has a chair that he or she always sits in, make sure that space is still available to them when the puppy is put away. Don't encroach on your other dog's areas because that will send the wrong signals to your dog. The puppy's space should be somewhere that your dog won't mind being blocked from visiting. Similarly, make sure that none of your dog's toys or other items end up in the puppy's space.

Before bringing your puppy home, you will need a neutral place for your dog and the puppy to meet, like a park within walking distance.

Your dog needs to meet the puppy in a place where possessive tendencies will not immediately kick in at the meeting. The last thing you want is for your dog to react territorially with your puppy. Making the initial meeting in a place that is familiar to your dog but that is not within your dog's territory will help make the meeting easier to manage. Once your dog and the puppy have the opportunity to sniff each other and get familiar with each other's scent, it will not be as much of a threat to bring the puppy home.

Schedule the meeting so that there are at least two adults present (you and another family member or a friend). The role of one adult will be to manage the puppy while the other helps keep the current dog calm during the meeting. It is very likely that one or both of the canines will be incredibly excited about the meeting, and it could quickly become

Photo Courtesy Of
Kay Patton

too much for one adult to handle. The person who runs the home and the people who will be responsible for taking care of the dog and the puppy should also be present. It will help teach your Miniature Goldendoodle the family hierarchy. It is best not to have young children at the initial meeting as there will be enough energy and excitement between the dog and the puppy.

There is no way to know how quickly your dog will acclimate to having a new puppy in the house, but you should plan for it to take a while. Even if your dog loves other canines and seems to enjoy the puppy, it is best to keep them apart for a couple of weeks until the new family member learns the house rules. It is going to take your dog a bit of time to get accustomed to the idea of having a puppy in the house, as well as losing some of the dedicated time that you usually spend together with him. You will be spending time with the puppy, leaving the dog on its own to watch or mope. Once the dogs seem comfortable together and your Miniature Goldendoodle is allowed to go into other locations, your dog is going to experience some stress. That puppy is going to be invading the dog's space and using the dog's things, which can be particularly stressful for older dogs.

If you already have more than one dog, you will need to be even more diligent about applying the rules, particularly at the initial meeting. There should be one adult per dog if at all possible. You should also consider the personality of each dog prior to the meeting. If you can, have the dogs meet the puppy one at a time to keep the puppy from feeling overstressed. The other dogs can stay in the vehicle or be kept at a distance so that each dog gets a chance to meet and sniff the puppy. This will give you time to gauge how each dog reacts to the puppy and how your puppy will handle each dog. This will also keep the puppy from being overwhelmed and keeps the dogs from being too excited—the excitement of one will be contagious to the rest, making for an incredibly boisterous encounter.

Dangerous Foods

CHECKLIST
Dangerous Foods Checklist

Here's a checklist that you can cut out and keep on your fridge of the most common human foods that are toxic for dogs:

- Onions, chives, garlic (very small amounts of garlic may be okay)
- Chocolate, especially dark chocolate
- Salty foods
- Fruit with pits like peaches, plums, and persimmons
- Coconut water; too much coconut oil
- Grapes, raisins, and currants
- Xylitol, an artificial sweetener found in things like gum and some low-fat peanut butter
- Coffee and other sources of caffeine
- Fried or fatty foods
- Alcohol
- Macadamia and other types of nuts
- Too much dairy (a small piece of cheese now and then may be okay)
- Raw yeast dough

Dogs that are as friendly as the Miniature Goldendoodle pose a real challenge in terms of food, and you really need to be aware of the foods that they should not eat, as should your children. It is going to be incredibly tempting to give the puppy food you are eating because it is easy to think that a small amount won't do much harm; however, it will. Even if the Miniature Goldendoodle is a medium-sized dog, they do like to eat well over their limit. You will need to make sure that your little one does not eat too much and become obese. Then there are a host of foods that your dog shouldn't eat because dogs don't digest all foods the same way people do. Most people know not to feed chocolate to dogs (even people who have never had one), but there are several foods that are far more dangerous.

The following is a list of foods that you need to make sure are never accessible to your sweet little Miniature Goldendoodle, no matter the age of your dog.

- Apple seeds
- Chocolate
- Coffee
- Cooked bones (they can kill when they splinter in the dog's mouth or stomach)
- Corn on the cob (it is the cob that is deadly to dogs; corn off the cob is fine, but you need to make sure that your Miniature Goldendoodle cannot reach any corn that is still on the cob)
- Grapes/raisins
- Macadamia nuts
- Onions and chives
- Peaches, persimmons, and plums

- Tobacco (your puppy will not know that it is not a food and may eat it if left out)
- Xylitol (a sugar substitute in candies and baked goods)
- Yeast

These are the foods that could be deadly to your puppy, but there are also foods that your dog shouldn't eat to stay healthy. Check out The Canine Journal list of foods and make sure that your family abides by the rules of your house in terms of what people food your dog is given.

No doubt, it is going to be difficult because you will want to share with those adorable, pleading puppy eyes. Even for safe foods, you should keep it to a minimum how much you share, with the recommendation being not to give your dog any human food. Dogs do not have the same metabolism as humans, and the highly processed people food is unhealthy for their digestive tracks. To keep your Miniature Goldendoodle healthy, stick to giving the puppy dog food or food that is meant for dogs, and keep all of the dangerous foods well out of reach.

Hazards To Fix

Puppy-proofing your home is going to be every bit as time consuming as it is to babyproof your home. With so many potentially dangerous items around the home, you are going to have to see the world from your Miniature Goldendoodle's perspective. Before your puppy's arrival, get down on your stomach in each room and look around for potential dangers.

Go through the following sections to get an idea of what you need to watch for during your inspection. Inspecting from your puppy's perspective will help you see the world from an entirely different point of view.

Start your puppy-proofing at least a month before your young canine's arrival. This will give you ample time to take care of everything.

Kitchen And Eating Areas

The kitchen is always one of the most dangerous areas for animals and children. There are poisons in the cabinets, sharp utensils, and a host of other things on which pets and kids can hurt themselves. Securing your kitchen area will be the same for your Miniature Goldendoodle puppy as it would be for a toddler. They do not tend to be troublemakers. They typically use their intelligence to make you happy, but that does not mean they won't try to entertain themselves. With all of the smells and food, the kitchen is a curiosity for puppies (and dogs). They will likely work their way into your cabinets if the cabinets are not secured. In addition to keeping hazardous foods out of reach of your puppy, you need to make sure poisons are always stored in a place where your Miniature Goldendoodle cannot get to it. Don't leave buckets with cleaning supplies in them or set cleaning supply bottles on the floor. All your puppy has to do is knock them over and spill the contents all over the floor. Get accustomed to storing all of your supplies in the cabinets where they are secure.

You also need to start putting your garbage can in a secure location. There will be a lot of things from the kitchen that end up in it, such as plastics, cooked chicken bones, broken glasses, and wrappers with interesting smells. Even a small Miniature Goldendoodle puppy will look for ways to tip the garbage can over and enjoy sniffing and eating the contents. Store your kitchen garbage can in the pantry or under the sink to ensure your small buddy cannot get to it.

Make sure there are no cords that will be within reach. Your teething puppy is likely to want to chew on them and see what happens when they pull on them. This is clearly an electrical danger, but that is not the only risk. When the cords are attached to objects like toaster ovens and blenders, this becomes very dangerous because they could crush the little pup. Keep all cords out of reach.

Bathroom And Laundry

The next most dangerous room for your puppy will be the bathroom, and it will require the same puppy-proofing that you did in the kitchen. All poisons need to be kept behind locked cabinet doors. Sharp objects need to be in locked drawers (except for the ones that are too high for a small dog to reach). Get used to keeping your toilet seat closed, and avoid using instant cleaners (you are going to need to get used to cleaning the toilets the old-fashioned way). Even if you keep the toilet seat closed, all it takes is a visitor leaving the lid up and your puppy could try to drink from it.

While not quite as dangerous as the kitchen and bathroom, the laundry room does have its share of potential puppy hazards. Laundry detergent and other cleaning supplies that you store in the laundry room need to be out of reach. If you have cabinets, make sure they are locked because they likely serve as storage for other items, and you do not want your puppy getting into them. If possible, find a way to keep clothing off of the floor. You don't want your little canine eating your dirty clothing or dragging your dirty undergarments around your home. There will also be times when items with potentially dangerous chemicals on them will be put in the dirty laundry, and you do not want those to be in within reach of your Miniature Goldendoodle. The easiest thing to do is to keep the laundry room door closed, but you should still make sure things are out of reach. You will probably let the puppy follow you into the room, and your attention will be elsewhere while the puppy is exploring.

Other Rooms

Just like you did in the kitchen, you are going to need to go around and make sure all electrical cords are off of the floor, cleaning products and dangerous items are out of reach, and there is nothing under furniture that could be dangerous to your puppy. This includes pens and pencils, which will probably look like chew toys to your puppy. You do not want your young dog getting sick from the graphite or pen ink, nor will you want to have to clean up the mess.

Photo Courtesy of
Kay Patton

Fireplaces need to be cleaned and all cleaning supplies stored out of reach, including items like pokers. Make sure that the interior is secured so that your Miniature Goldendoodle cannot enter it.

Have gates for stairs to keep your puppy from tumbling down them. It is best in the first months to avoid the stairs with your little puppy. Miniature Goldendoodles as adults are small; their puppies are tiny. To avoid them falling down the stairs, just keep them away from the stairs. You may want to plan to have a training session with any stairs you have inside your home once your puppy is a bit older.

If you have a cat, make sure the litter box is in a location that your puppy cannot reach. It won't need to be too high off the ground, but it does need to be secured away from your puppy. You will want to make sure your cat has time to learn the new location before the puppy arrives too. The last thing you should do to a cat is change where its restroom is located while it is coping with a new, energetic puppy.

Garage

Garages are a terribly dangerous place for any dog, but especially small puppies. They are going to be able to get into areas that you had not even considered. Under work benches and cars, in small spaces, and through holes you didn't know were there, puppies will find all of the most dangerous places without even trying.

It is best to keep your Miniature Goldendoodle out of the garage. If your puppy does go into the garage, never leave your small friend alone in there. Since you will likely be taking your Miniature Goldendoodle through the garage occasionally, it is best to puppy-proof it too.

Equipment, tools, car parts, and yard supplies all need to be stored off the ground and where the puppy cannot reach. Fortunately, that is relatively easy since your puppy is not going to get too big. This includes bike tools, leaf blowers, and other tools that you don't want your Miniature Goldendoodle chewing on if you are hanging out in the garage. Fishing equipment also needs to be organized and stored where your puppy will not eat your bait or get hurt on hooks. Make sure nothing is dangling over any countertops either.

Get down low and look around to see what all may be a potential danger to a young dog. Block any small areas where your puppy could potentially crawl, move wires and cables up out of reach, and store chemicals and tools that puppies and children should not touch.

Outdoors And Fencing

Never leave your Miniature Goldendoodle unattended in your yard, even if you have a fence. First, your dog is not going to like being away from everyone. Second, there are far too many dangerous things in the yard for a puppy or young dog.

As long as you never send your pup out alone, it should be relatively easy to puppy-proof the yard. Set aside an hour or two (depending on the yard size) to look it over and make sure the usual hazards are out of reach. Fertilizer, gardening tools, and power tools should all be stored in the garage or shed. Look over the fencing for holes near the ground, or places where a puppy may be able to burrow out. This includes looking for breaks that could trap your Miniature Goldendoodle. Also, if there is water in your backyard, such as a pool or small pond, make sure your puppy cannot get to it. Also check for poisonous plants and make them inaccessible to your puppy.

Determine where you want your Miniature Goldendoodle to use the restroom outside. This is going to be incredibly important because it will make the clean-up much easier. Make sure that the location is safe (no holes in the ground that could hurt the puppy and no cleaning supplies). There shouldn't be anything large and potentially dangerous in the area, such as a birdbath. An excited puppy or child may knock them over while playing. Your Miniature Goldendoodle is going to learn really quickly where to go to the bathroom if you stay consistent, and you want to make sure there are no risky items in the area.

Spend time walking around the yard checking it out. You should do this several times over the course of the month, keeping an eye out for anything that needs to be moved or fixed.

Supplies And Tools To Purchase And Prepare

After securing the inside and outside of your home, you can start the more enjoyable chores—buying things for your new dog. There are a number of things you will need before your Miniature Goldendoodle arrives. Create a checklist of everything you know you will need, and anything you think would be beneficial. Even if you don't buy anything extra, there are a lot of items that are basic needs for your puppy. The following list can help you get started:

- Crate
- Bed
- Leash
- Doggy Bags For Walks
- Collar
- Tags
- Puppy Food
- Water And Food Bowls (Sharing A Water Bowl Is Usually Ok, But Your Puppy Needs His Or Her Own Food Dish If You Have Multiple Dogs)
- Toothbrush
- Brush
- Toys

You can add anything else you want for your puppy to the list—this is just a starting point.

Items like training tools and treats should be on that list at some point, even if you don't buy them for the first week or two. You just need to determine which ones you want to use with your puppy. A combination of treats and toys will have the best results because you will not want to continually give your puppy extra food. You will also need to get equipment for training indoors for the first few weeks. Toys will need to be the right fit for your Miniature Goldendoodle puppy's little mouth. Don't get anything too big or heavy. Be aware that your little friend is going to follow you around, making it easy to work training and play into any time of day. It will build up your puppy's stamina though, so plan to increase playtime to both keep your puppy from boredom and in shape.

Planning The First Year's Budget

While they aren't nearly as expensive as newborn humans, puppies can be relatively costly. Setting up your budget before the puppy arrives will make sure that you can afford the things you need over the course of the year. This will include things like vet visits for shots, monthly heartworm pills, training supplies, and food. Make sure to include a cushion in the budget because it always costs more than you expect.

Start the budget as soon as you decide to get a Miniature Goldendoodle. They may not require much extra for their care (you are their favorite source of entertainment, so you aren't going to need to constantly find ways to keep them from boredom), and they are small, but all dogs cost a lot their first year as you learn what they need. You are also going to need to do a good bit of research for your Miniature Goldendoodle. Vets have different prices depending on where you live, and you want one with a great reputation, as well as knowledge about designer breeds. Because they have much shorter histories, the types of typical health problems vary much more for designer breeds than purebred dogs; however, they have an easier history to track than mutts. You want a vet who can address the potential issues common with designer breeds.

Summary

Your Miniature Goldendoodle's focus is pretty much going to be around you and your family. They are intelligent, but they do not tend to cause the kinds of problems that Corgis and other intelligent dogs cause because Miniature Goldendoodles find all the entertainment they need with their people. This makes them incredibly entertaining and enjoyable to have around. In those first few months though, they are going to be learning everything, and that means investing more time to keep them safe and happy. To make sure you aren't distracted, make sure you have everything set up well ahead of your Miniature Goldendoodle's arrival.

Make sure that your whole family, including your other pets, is prepared for the new arrival. Have the day of the introduction already planned out, particularly with young kids and dogs. Spend some extra time with your current pets so that they do not feel like they are being replaced. You need to plan to spend extra time with them after the puppy's arrival too because they will feel left out while you are training and playing with the puppy. Take longer walks or plan to spend more time playing in the yard. Make time in your schedule now to do that once the puppy arrives because it will be much harder to work it into your schedule later. Having something familiar will help your dog adjust faster to the little puppy.

CHAPTER 6
The First Week

With the arrival of your Miniature Goldendoodle, everything in your personal life is going to be different. These dogs are more than happy to integrate into your family as quickly and seamlessly as possible. They will pay attention to everything you do and will try to find a way to make you happy, whether through cuddling or playing. Puppies are a bit more of a challenge, but even they want to be with you as much as possible. Time is going to fly by, and before you know it your puppy or young dog is going to be a full-fledged member of your family, going everywhere you go. You probably won't even notice how quickly your dog becomes an integral part of your family.

HELPFUL TIP
Now's the Time to Check Out Pet Insurance

Pet insurance can help you recover some of the costs if your dog suffers from an expensive injury or serious illness. Plans don't cover preexisting conditions, and most plans also have waiting periods before coverage begins, so the time to sign up for pet insurance is while your dog is still a puppy.

One thing to remember about your Miniature Goldendoodle is that the dog's abilities reflect the time and effort you put into the training, and it requires a commitment on your part to make sure your pup remains happy and healthy.

That first week will establish a lot about your relationship and the way your puppy feels about your home. From the beginning, the hard work will start to pay off (puppy-proofing a home is definitely hard work) as your puppy begins to explore your home. However, you are going to need to train your new little friend every day, something that will be increasingly difficult as you get busier. No matter how crammed your schedule is, make the time to do some training every day so that your puppy doesn't get into trouble as an adult for doing the things you used to think were cute.

Preparation And Planning

If the last chapter taught you anything, it was that planning and preparation begin long before your new dog arrives. Everything needs to be set up before your Miniature Goldendoodle comes home so that the transition for everyone in the household goes smoother.

The day before your Miniature Goldendoodle arrives, do a final check of your home. Your puppy is going to be curious, so you should get down on your hands and knees and really inspect every room for potential hazards from the puppy's angle.

Have a list of everything your puppy will need right from the start. That list should include the following (the list is not comprehensive):

- Food
- Bed
- Crate
- Toys
- Water and food dishes
- Leash
- Collar
- Treats

If you want to fence off a small area for the puppy, make sure you know how to work the gates. You will also need to test the fencing for your little one to make sure it isn't easy to knock over.

Sit down with the family and make sure everyone understands the rules, particularly children. Proper puppy handling is essential for making sure your children and puppy play well together, and that does mean being strict with your children—not just your new pup. Verify that everyone knows their roles—who will walk the puppy, who will feed and monitor the water bowl, and who will participate in daily training. Training should be everyone's job, but one person should be responsible for the harder tasks, such as teaching the dog to sit and stay, and that should be a daily task for one person. Others are free to join in, but having a primary trainer who handles it daily helps establish consistency. One adult should be involved with the puppy's care too. Pairing up gives your children a chance to be responsible with a bit of extra help until they can remember to do it on their own. One adult and one child can monitor the water bowl; one adult and child can feed the puppy. This makes it easier to ensure that nothing important in the care of the new family member is forgotten in the early days.

Finally, your Miniature Goldendoodle requires a routine in the early days. It is fine if that schedule changes later on, but establishing a predictable schedule in the first few weeks or months helps the puppy feel safe and secure in the new home. It is also fine to occasionally change up the schedule a little, and you can tweak it as your puppy gets more com-

Photo Courtesy Of
Nicole Chapple

fortable. The schedule will help you as much as the puppy; if you have a routine, you are less likely to forget a task—autopilot can be a beautiful thing when training a puppy. Your young friend will also become a little alarm after you have been following the schedule long enough.

The final week before your puppy arrives should be used to review everything one last time. Develop the training schedule, starting with when you get up and need to make time for walking, to when you go to bed. You know that things will change, but once you are accustomed to the schedule (if only a little) it will make things easier after your puppy comes home.

The Ride Home

After you meet your new companion, it is time to start training. Everything that your puppy should learn has the foundation in that first car ride home. You are going to want to cuddle the little canine (especially if the puppy is scared in the car), but you have got to start being consistent from that first encounter. Your puppy is learning from what you do and say during those early days, and you want the impression to be friendly and consistent. Those adorable eyes will stare you down, and if you give in and take the puppy out of the crate, things are only going to get harder to change as that will be the expectation from that moment. That adorable little face hides an intelligent mind, and if your Miniature Goldendoodle knows that you are weak to the puppy-dog eyes, they are going to use that against you.

It is best to have two adults on the trip to pick up the puppy so that one person can give attention to the puppy while the other person drives. The Miniature Goldendoodle likely will not be too afraid, but you should provide assurance to your new friend because of all of the changes to the puppy's life. The more positive the driving experience to your home is, the more your new puppy will enjoy future car rides. This is a great way to introduce your new dog to car trips, an activity that is likely to become a regular part of your and your dog's schedule as you go out for new adventures, hikes, and excursions.

Ensure the crate is secure in the car so that your Miniature Goldendoodle is not sliding around in the back area. The crate should be secured, and not held in someone's lap. The puppy should experience minimal jostling to create a positive experience.

First Night Frights

That first night is always difficult for new puppies. It is the first night away from the mother and the familiar comforts that the puppy has known, and it is understandably a scary experience. However, there is only so much you can do comfort the little one without undercutting yourself. What you do not want is for your puppy to think that negative behavior will get the desired results. You will need to work through those first few nights to teach your puppy that it is not as scary as it seems and that your home is a safe place.

If you have a policy that keeps dogs off of the bed, don't let the puppy on the bed. You cannot bring the puppy into your room to sleep after he becomes vocal about his fears because that will encourage whimpering and whining every night until that action is repeated. It is nearly impossible to convince a Miniature Goldendoodle that something is not allowed if you allow it once. Keep in mind they are intelligent, and they will figure out how they got you to do what they wanted. Then they will repeat it.

Because of the number of strange noises and smells, your new companion is going to feel uncertain in your home. As a result, the puppy will probably make a lot of noises, including whimpering, and that adorable little face is going to work against you and make you want to give in to what the little charmer wants. You need to expect this so that you can be strong. Learning to ignore the noises from your puppy—and not looking at your puppy when you hear them—makes training considerably easier.

Photo Courtesy Of
Denise Peek

Do not move your Miniature Goldendoodle just because you don't want to deal with the noises. Ignoring puppies long enough for a few days will convince them to stop. Having your new canine sleep a long way from you will terrify the puppy and will be proof that the puppy is alone in your home—fears you do not want to instill (let alone confirm). Even if your puppy wants more attention and closeness, keeping the Miniature Goldendoodle in the designated space over the first week will show the dog that it is not alone, but there are rules to follow.

Expect that you won't get much sleep in those early days. After all, you do have a small, furry baby to tend to that will require love and care. It is all part of what you sacrifice to start with a puppy instead of an older dog. The designated Miniature Goldendoodle sleep space proves that your puppy has a place—even if your new young friend has no interest in having his own personal space. There may be times where your puppy will want to have a little alone time after being overstimulated. Boundaries help the new pup understand the restrictions too. Over time, you can let the puppy explore, but for now, the Miniature Goldendoodle should be kept in an area where the puppy can learn to be comfortable. You need to go into that space often as your puppy won't want to be alone. Do have another area nearby for the puppy to use the bathroom. If you want to start by training your puppy to only use the restroom outside, you are going to have to get accustomed to sleeping even less as you will need to take the puppy outside several times during your normal sleep hours.

First Vet Visit

The first vet visit is definitely something that you and the puppy will both face with trepidation. Still, you need to do it within the first day or two of the dog's arrival at your home. It is necessary to ensure that your little one is healthy, as well as creating that initial bond between the vet and your puppy. Considering the fact that Miniature Goldendoodles are a designer dog, you need the baseline to ensure that your puppy is growing up well. Even though your puppy is not going to be happy about it, getting familiar with the vet is important. As an outgoing, friendly dog, your Miniature Goldendoodle will probably develop a great relationship with the vet over time.

The vet will conduct the initial assessment and gain a baseline of your puppy's health. As your new little companion grows you will be able to make sure it follows the expected health milestones.

For that first visit, your puppy will probably want to explore the waiting room, including meeting everyone there. You will need to be careful that your puppy does not get too hyperactive or close to other animals, especially with older animals that are not interested in being pestered by a puppy. Ask everyone before letting the puppy approach any other animal in the waiting room. Many of the pets are likely to be there for an ailment and may not be feeling well enough to entertain a young dog.

Praise your pup with positive feedback for good behavior. Anything your puppy does that you want continued should be praised—this will have a much greater effect than any kind of food because your attention and happiness are what your Miniature Goldendoodle wants. This will help your little canine to get more comfortable with the environment so that future visits are not as scary. The positive attention also gives your puppy a more positive impression of that first vet visit, giving your puppy a reason to look forward to future trips too.

The Start Of Training

Photo Courtesy Of Bianca Barron

Training starts the second your puppy gets in the car, but you have a lot of time-intensive work ahead of you. Training may not be particularly hard for Miniature Goldendoodles, but they may look for ways to persuade you that you have better things to do than to train them. That cute little face and adorable expression can easily distract you from the behaviors you need your puppy to learn. Over the next few weeks and months, you need to establish some basic training foundations.

Barking

Some Miniature Goldendoodles may be a little more vocal than expected, but you can train them out of this habit. They are prone to barking on walks and when they see or hear something outside. Start training your puppy not to bark at random sounds and sights, starting during that first week. It may mean a few extra treats (make sure to take treats on the walk), but that is all right in the early days and will help your puppy to be quieter.

Your Miniature Goldendoodle may also be a bit noisier in an effort to get your attention. The best way to discourage this is to ignore your puppy when this happens. That does mean you will be training yourself as well as the puppy, so it will probably take time as you figure out when the puppy is barking for your attention or for some other reason. You can prioritize and start by discouraging random barking first, and then stop giving as much attention when the barking is reduced when walking.

The Leash

Leash training should be incredibly easy, but keep in mind that it is not exactly natural. Depending on your puppy's personality, the leash may be treated like a chew toy, so you will need to train the new pup not to do that. Mostly your puppy is happy to be included in whatever you are doing. Do be careful not to be too forceful on the leash, and plan to take short walks in the beginning. A trip around the block is fine for the first few days. The puppy is going to be taking in the new world, so the walks are not going to be real exercise until your little canine is a good bit older.

Teaching Respect

Miniature Goldendoodles will need to be taught to respect all of the family members, even if the dog is very personable. If not trained properly, your puppy could start to act like a little terror, disregarding family members and barking incessantly. You aren't likely to need to worry about more serious problems, but you don't want your Miniature Goldendoodle to act like a brat when it gets older.

Consistency

The best way to gain a Miniature Goldendoodle's respect is through consistent training. You should not use fear to do this—your puppy wants to please you, that is the best leverage for teaching it respect too. It wants to have positive attention, so just be consistent in your approach, and almost everything else should be easy.

The reason to bring this up is because it is easy to give in to those puppy-dog eyes and pleading face. You will have to be strong, but as long as you are consistent, your Miniature Goldendoodle will be easy to train.

Acclimation To The Home

Photo Courtesy Of Mindy Parks

Any rules you want your puppy to learn will need to be applied consistently, no matter who the family member with the dog is. This means making sure everyone follows the rules. The one common problem that you do have to watch is being consistent. It will take a while for your puppy to understand that the rules will not change. Being consistent and not allowing bending or breaking of those rules is the best way to get your puppy acclimated to your home.

CHAPTER 7
The First Month

Making it through the first week is the biggest challenge, and it will set you up for the remainder of that first month. Using the things that worked well can help streamline the processes and training. You have been learning as much as your Miniature Goldendoodle, and now you have an idea of what works, what doesn't, and how your puppy will try to break the rules.

Training a Miniature Goldendoodle is comparatively easy compared to most other breeds. Their intelligence combined with their love of being in a pack make them easy to train. They are not known for testing boundaries or being destructive when they are bored, something that many intelligent dogs tend to do. If there are tricks you want your Miniature Goldendoodle to learn, make sure you plan for it because you may be able to get started during the first month.

Photo Courtesy Of
Sophia Georgantonis

Not Up To Full Strength

As a puppy, your Miniature Goldendoodle won't be able to do the kind of activities that you probably look forward to doing together once the puppy matures. All of that energy and excitement is quickly used up as the little one explores the house, backyard, and a small portion of the neighborhood. For this month, walks will be short. Exercise should be broken up over the course of the day because your small friend will not be able to sustain long periods of continuous activities. Sleeps will be frequent once those energy reserves are used up. A few short walks and some energetic playing will be more than enough to keep your puppy too tired to be any real trouble.

The ratio of nap to play will be fairly equal, giving you more time to do other things as your pup sleeps. Puppy naps should always take place in the puppy area—no exceptions. Sometimes emergencies happen, and when they do, if your puppy naps in a different area, you have to be ready to drop everything you are doing once the dog wakes up.

After the first month, your Miniature Goldendoodle will have considerably more stamina—you will probably feel like it has doubled. You will be able to take longer walks (although not a full walk quite yet) and play and training sessions will last longer. Plan to adjust your routine to reflect the increased energy and needs of the young dog. You can reduce the number of walks as you make them longer. Training sessions can last 5, 10, or 15 minutes longer than they did in the first week.

Setting The Rules And Sticking To Them

Intelligent dogs are observant. Failing to be consistent is something they will notice, and they will take advantage of it. Deviation from the schedule or the norm, if it is in their favor, they are going to try to keep that going. This is certainly true with Miniature Goldendoodles; they will use any weakness toward their sweet temperament and adorable appearance that you have to their advantage.

Fortunately, their idea of taking advantage of you is to get more food from your plate or stay in bed a little longer. What they want is not going to be nefarious; in fact, it will mostly line up with the things you will probably want to do. Unlike other intelligent dogs, Miniature Goldendoodles largely focus on getting more time and attention from their people. But you will have to make sure that you stick to established rules and schedules so that they are not only happy but healthy. Don't get in the habit of feeding them from your plate. Enforce training, even if your Miniature

Goldendoodle does not seem interested. By acting excited, your emotions will transfer to the puppy.

Despite the easygoing temperament, your Miniature Goldendoodle needs to know that you are the one in control. They may not be inclined to act like an alpha dog, but you don't want them disregarding you either. They will try to convince you that they need more attention, more food, less strict rules, and less training, but they need to know that these things are important. Your Miniature Goldendoodle will be inclined to keep to the rules, which is why you have to make a concerted effort to keep it up. You will quickly feel complacent with the training as you see the results fairly early on. If you have certain training goals, make sure to keep them up over the course of your Miniature Goldendoodle's training.

Early Socialization

HELPFUL TIP

Socialization is Key

While Golden Retrievers tend to be very friendly with everybody, Toy Poodles often need more time to warm up to people. That's why socialization is key for Miniature Goldendoodles, so they learn to trust other people and dogs and become familiar with new environments. This helps them grow up to be friendly, confident dogs.

Early socialization is important even for a puppy known for being friendly and gregarious. The socialization ensures that your young dog enjoys the company of other dogs. Socialization is an incredibly important activity that you should focus on during the first few months of your young canine's arrival. If your family and friends have dogs, ask them to meet up for some puppy playtime. Play dates with dogs you already know will give you a much better environment than a dog park and help you in keeping control over the situation. Socialization could even be built into your walks if you know enough of the neighbors and their dogs.

It is equally important to socialize your puppy with people. This task is also easier as people are more predictable in how they react to dogs. With a sweet Miniature Goldendoodle that is going to be incredibly easy—walking the puppy is going to attract people who want to pet the young one, particularly children. You will need to monitor children more closely in their interactions to make sure they are not too rough. Also, let people know that you do not want the puppy picked up. That way the puppy is not accidentally hurt while socializing. Getting hurt will have the opposite effect to the one you want as the Miniature Goldendoodle will learn to be more wary and fearful.

Socialization should be something that you do several times a week, or daily if possible. The more socialized your little canine is, the more activities you will be able to enjoy with them later without worrying about how your Miniature Goldendoodle will react.

Do be kind to any older dogs that you encounter. An energetic little puppy is probably more than they can handle, and you do not want to make them feel uneasy. This is particularly true if you have an older dog yourself. Make sure that your older canine gets some dedicated alone time with you and a lot of time away from the new arrival. If your older dog is irritable, you may want to keep the puppy away most to all of the time.

Photo Courtesy Of
Sarah Duncan

Treats And Rewards Vs. Punishments

Photo Courtesy Of
Lucy Ciprian

Most people think treats are an essential part of training, but with dogs like Miniature Goldendoodles, that is absolutely not necessary after a month or two of training. They react just as well to positive rewards as they do to treats. Since Miniature Goldendoodles are food motivated it will be tempting to continue to use food as a reward. However, their intelligence and desire to please mean that positive reinforcement is going to be one of the best rewards. Praising your new companion for doing well, providing extra attention and cuddle time, and bringing out new toys will be just as much of a motivator as any treat you can offer. Save the treats for tricks and other unnecessary training that you want to do later.

Exercise—Encouraging Staying Active

Photo Courtesy Of
Jillian Wise

Your Miniature Goldendoodle will require at least 30 minutes of solid exercise to stay fit, and more time if your dog is on the larger side of the breed. This probably won't be particularly difficult as it gives you a chance to exercise with your dog. Playing with them will also be incredibly easy to do as most of them will love to retrieve toys during play.

Best Activities

Because they love to be around people, there are a lot of activities that will make your puppy happy. All of the games that you think about when playing with a dog, like fetch and tug of war, will be very welcome for your little buddy. As long as there is no running involved, you can play games in the house too, which is great during the summer and winter when your puppy may get too hot or cold while playing outside. In addition to no running in the house, make sure that there are no hard toys being thrown. You don't want things to get broken. However, small, light toys can be thrown low to the ground for your little puppy to chase. Keep away is another fun game if there are at least a couple of people available to participate.

CHAPTER 8
Housetraining

Housetraining is usually one of the things that make people decide not to bring a puppy into their home. It is not something that most people enjoy doing, but it is necessary. With the Miniature Goldendoodle it is slightly less of a chore than it is with many other breeds. Not that it will be a picnic, it just isn't likely to take as long as you might expect.

Before getting started, here are a couple of things to keep in mind about training.

1. Miniature Goldendoodle puppies should never be allowed to roam your home freely. When the puppy is out of the puppy area, he should have constant supervision. That will lower the risk that the little one will have an accident. Nor is your Miniature Goldendoodle puppy going to want to be in a soiled crate or area, so this will simplify housetraining.

2. Your puppy needs to have easy access to the locations where you have determined it is acceptable for him to use the restroom. Having a designated puppy area will help. However, if this is not possible, be prepared for frequent trips outside.

These are two key rules you will have to enforce. To help you be consistent, here are the things you need to consider before your Miniature Goldendoodle puppy arrives.

Understanding Your Dog

As a people-loving dog, your Miniature Goldendoodle is going to stay with you as much as possible—they aren't big on being individuals and do not care to be alone. Still, they are an intelligent dog, and just because a Miniature Goldendoodle doesn't go to the bathroom outside does not mean that he does not understand that the outdoors is the right place. Often if he doesn't go outside it is because the Miniature Goldendoodle is opting for convenience because you aren't being consistent. As the adult, you are responsible for not only teaching your puppy what is the right thing to do, but making sure that you provide all of the necessary opportunities to do the right thing.

Your young friend can learn how to use a doggy door, although this breed may not be keen on going outside alone. It may not be worth the installation if your young pup prefers that you to go outside too. You should probably start with taking your Miniature Goldendoodle outside on a leash during the early phases. If you decide to use puppy pads, you need to understand that you will have to move the training outdoors relatively early as your puppy will learn fast. Puppy pads are a nice transition, but it really should not take too long. Leaving puppy pads inside for too long could give your small companion the wrong idea that it is all right to do its business inside.

Given their intelligence and desire to please, it is your job to provide the opportunities and consistency in the early phases to ensure that your Miniature Goldendoodle learns. Plenty of positive reinforcement will go a long way toward making your puppy trainable, and will make your life easier.

Inside Or Outside

Naturally, you want to train your Miniature Goldendoodle to go outside as soon as possible, but young puppies don't quite understand that in the first few weeks—not until you train them. This could mean that you need to start with indoor training for the short term. This will be especially true if it is cold when your new puppy arrives at your home, so plan accordingly. If you do start training indoors, make sure your puppy understands that there is only one place where it is all right to go, and be consistent with that approach.

HELPFUL TIP

Crate Training

Crate training can not only help with house-training your puppy, but it can set him up for a lifetime of being comfortable in a crate. Even if you don't intend to crate your dog on a regular basis, it should be comfortable in one in case it ever needs to spend time in a crate, such as in a vet clinic, boarding facility, grooming salon, or during travel.

If you are able to start training outdoors, you should already have a place chosen for your puppy to go. Now it is time for you to plan frequent (very frequent) trips outside, including at night when you would normally be asleep. It is incredibly time consuming, but as long as you are consistent in your approach, your little pooch will start to understand. The first month or so will be rough, but ultimately entirely worth the effort. Though you will need to stay with your young dog, your puppy will love it, which will make going outside a great experience. Just make sure to stay positive while you are out there, and don't distract your puppy. Having one place for your puppy to go in the yard not only helps to get the idea across that this is the place to use the bathroom, it makes it easier for you to clean up behind your companion every week. Naturally, you will likely want somewhere close to the door because you won't want your puppy to hold it too long. It is also good to have somewhere close to the door in winter as the Miniature Goldendoodle is going to want to keep restroom outings as short as possible. The poor little guy simply was not built for cold weather.

Photo Courtesy Of
Sarah Jones

They Are Pleasures—But You Still Need To Be Consistent

There are so many great things about Miniature Goldendoodles. They are friendly, positive, energetic without being overwhelming, great cuddlers, and potentially quick learners. Fail to be consistent and you are going to find that last aspect to be false, but it isn't the dog's fault—it's yours. Your Miniature Goldendoodle wants to have fun with you and wants you to be happy, but the puppy always doesn't want to do anything that isn't fun. If you let your puppy get away with something once, that sends the wrong message, and that is not something you want to do with housetraining. That does not mean that you should shout at your canine if an accident happens, but it does mean you need to put more time into getting him outside and focusing on puppy business first.

Photo Courtesy Of Ashley Stella

On rough days, fight the urge to feel that your puppy's action is good enough or close enough. They need the rules to always apply, and only that is good enough.

This applies to everyone in the family who is helping with the housetraining. If you want to use a word to tell your puppy when to use the restroom, everyone in the family will need to use that word. If you plan to take the little guy outside once an hour during the day and several times at night, you will need to do it at the same time, or a member of your family will need to take the puppy outside at that time. If there is a single area in the yard, everyone in the family needs to take the puppy there. This kind of consistency is what can make the training go smoother.

Positive Reinforcement—It's About Respect

After the puppy uses the restroom, you can either give a treat or play with him for a little bit. The treat will be nice, but you should use it sparingly. Little dogs can get overweight very quickly. With a Miniature Goldendoodle puppy, the playtime will actually be more of a reward than the treat. If that puppy knows that a certain action will mean more playtime, there are very good odds that your small friend will be entirely eager to use the restroom (though it may take a while to understand that he should only do that outside). The puppy will begin to look up to you because it will be obvious that you are in charge. It is a type of respect, although not the kind that you get from working dogs. For the Miniature Goldendoodle, it is more about playing and being with you, and if the little dog knows that something makes you unhappy or upset, avoiding that behavior is a pretty good incentive.

Consistency is obviously required for your Miniature Goldendoodle to understand what is expected. They are smart, but not quite as intelligent as a Corgi or a working dog. Miniature Goldendoodles aren't driven by wanting a clean living space or doing what the alpha of the pack says; they are more interested in playing and having fun, or cuddling. This means you don't have to worry as much about them doing something to test you as to do something because you haven't been consistent, which is why it is so important to know how you are going to reward your Miniature Goldendoodle.

During the day, you can reward a successful trip outside by playing for a few minutes. At night, a successful trip could result in a small treat (you don't want the puppy to be hyperactive anyway, so it is probably best to avoid nighttime play). Over time, you will be able to go outside less often, and your small canine will understand that these trips outside

71

are the times to use the bathroom. At some point, your little companion will even understand that you should be told when it is time to go outside (if there is too large a gap between outings). Yes, this is still a long way away, but it is the goal.

You want to build a positive relationship with your Miniature Goldendoodle, so punishing your puppy for accidents is discouraged. Miniature Goldendoodles are smart, but they may not understand the correlation between the waste and the punishment. In the end, the puppy's takeaway is that it should use the bathroom some place where you can't find it inside.

The Miniature Goldendoodle wants you to be happy—you are more fun to be with when you are. They want to enjoy their time with you, so positive reinforcement is the best way to give your young pup attention and is a great motivator.

Regular Schedule, Doggy Door, Or Newspaper?

Determining the best way to get your puppy to go outside can be a challenge, and a lot of it depends on your schedule. If you cannot be home to take your little doggy out about once an hour, you will probably have to start with puppy pads.

The Recommendation

It is best to train your young one outside, even if there is some indoor training in the beginning. Making the kind of time required to do this in the early days can turn the training into an activity similar to a full-time job, but that is part of the price you pay for having a young dog you get to train and bond with from the beginning. Ultimately, the goal is to have the puppy only use the restroom outside, so you want to minimize how long a young pup is allowed to use the bathroom inside your home. The longer you wait to move the training outside, the harder it will be for your Miniature Goldendoodle to understand why the rules have changed.

How To Transition To The Outdoors

If you have to start with some indoor training (particularly in winter), you can start moving the training outside a little bit at a time. Place a small puppy pad in the area where you want the puppy to start doing its business in your yard, but also work to train your young pup that it is all right to go on other things outside too. After a while, you can get rid of the puppy pad inside, teaching your young buddy that it is no longer OK to go in your home.

Leash training is also a great way to transition. Having the leash indicates to your little friend that it is time to do some business. Then you can either go for a walk or out to the backyard. The puppy will know that this is a sign to go, and then enjoy the rest of the time outside.

It's All On You—Miniature Goldendoodles Just Want To Please

Miniature Goldendoodles are people pleasers—they want everyone around them to be happy, and that is really all it takes for them to be content. They can be incredibly easy to train, so you probably are not looking at the kind of nightmare experience that makes some people decide not to adopt a puppy. As long as you are consistent and positive, your puppy will figure it out and start doing things your way.

If your Miniature Goldendoodle continues to do its business inside, you need to examine how you and the family have been training the puppy. It is likely that there is an inconsistent approach or mixed signals. That doesn't mean pointing fingers, but it does mean making sure everyone understands that they need to work the same way. When Miniature Goldendoodles don't learn something, there is usually another problem causing the puppy to fail to learn.

CHAPTER 9
Socialization And Experience

Socialization is essential for every dog, even one as famously friendly as the Miniature Goldendoodle. It is possible that smaller Miniature Goldendoodles could develop small dog syndrome if they aren't properly trained and socialized. Even individual dogs that are on the larger spectrum of the breed's size need to be socialized so that they can be as happy and friendly outside your home as they are inside.

All dogs, regardless of breed, have to learn how to interact with other canines and humans. You should create time in your schedule to ensure that your dog receives socialization to bring out those fantastic personality traits. If you begin socialization when your puppy is still young, he will learn that other dogs and people can be a lot of fun.

Benefits Of Socialization

Socialization is a critical training aspect of your Miniature Goldendoodle's curriculum because small dog syndrome is difficult for both the dog and the family. As the syndrome's name suggests, small dogs may develop behavioral problems if they aren't properly socialized. While it is not common in Miniature Goldendoodles, if your puppy isn't socialized or trained to behave it is possible this will be a problem when your dog reaches maturity. Small dogs are often treated differently than larger dogs because of their size. You are more likely to allow bad behavior for a puppy or a small dog, which trains them that they can get away with inappropriate behavior. Because of the intelligence of this breed, you could be creating significant problems for yourself and your dog later on.

If your dog develops small dog syndrome, the dog may end up bullying other dogs by barking incessantly at them or by being aggressive. The small dog may also feel afraid of other, larger dogs, which could make going outside very hard to deal with for both of you. Either way, neither you nor your dog will be happy when not at home.

Even if your pup isn't small, you don't want him to be unnecessarily afraid when you go out in public, and you definitely don't want your dog to be a prolific barker. Despite being a fantastic breed, individual Miniature Goldendoodles can become difficult to handle if not properly socialized. The guidance helps them learn about other dogs and people, instead of letting them learn to fear these encounters. The socialization also helps your little buddy learn not to be skittish or mistrustful. Getting out of the home is great for every dog, no matter how much they love to be home. This is why you need to make sure that you teach your puppy that the world is a safe place so that going outside is a reason for excitement.

It's Easy

HELPFUL TIP
Fear-Aggression

While Golden Retrievers tend to be very friendly with everybody, Toy Poodles often need more time to warm up to people. That's why socialization is key for Miniature Goldendoodles, so they learn to trust other people and dogs and become familiar with new environments. This helps them grow up to be friendly, confident dogs.

Since this is a breed that loves people and dogs, socialization is fairly easy. Their intelligence means that what you teach them in those first few trips outside will already start to make your puppy feel more comfortable when going out. They usually love being with people and dogs, so there is already a lot to work with—mostly you are encouraging their natural temperament by providing a safe and friendly environment. As your Miniature Goldendoodle ages, you will be able to do more and experience a much wider variety of adventures. However, in those early days, you want to keep the socialization of your pooch manageable (instead of overwhelming) and the environment predictable.

It will probably be incredibly easy to socialize your puppy with people because people are going to want to play with such an adorable dog. You will be responsible for ensuring that the people who want to interact with your young pooch understand how to play responsibly with your newest family member. This is particularly true when it comes to picking up your puppy or trying to give the canine people food. Make sure people who want to play with your little dog understand that you are training your puppy, so they need to abide by the rules for playing with him. All playing with the puppy should be done on his level, which most people will do automatically—most people don't go picking up someone else's dog. However, it is always a good idea to make sure that people know that so that your puppy can really enjoy the experience.

Problems Arising From Lack Of Socialization—Small Dog Syndrome

The primary problem with any small dog is the risk of small dog syndrome if the puppy is not socialized when he is young. It isn't a life-threatening ailment, but it can reduce your dog's quality of life (not to mention yours). It isn't too likely to happen with this breed, but you should still take the necessary steps to socialize your dog so that he isn't one of the rare statistics.

Photo Courtesy Of Linda Jasso

Small dog syndrome is a problem that develops in small breeds because they are treated differently than larger dogs. People tend to be overprotective of small dogs to keep them safe. It is typically unnecessary, but it is difficult to fight the natural urge to protect them since they are so small. Not only are you likely to be overprotective, you will probably let your puppy get away with more bad behavior. This is dangerous no matter what size of dog, but especially for intelligent ones. Letting your puppy jump on people will be a problem as your dog gets older and it isn't so cute. If your canine remains small, you are more likely to let them get away with inappropriate behavior well into adulthood, which could cause problems, particularly if you have larger dogs that think they can behave that way too.

Large Miniature Goldendoodles aren't likely to be overprotected, but you still need to be careful when they are young since you do not know for certain how big they will be once they are full grown.

You should always consistently apply the rules, no matter the size of your puppy and dog. As an intelligent canine, the Miniature Goldendoodle learns that bad behavior will be acceptable from those early days if you don't apply the rules consistently. If you are protective of your puppy, that smart little dog is going to learn to fear those things. Instead of keeping your puppy isolated, let the little guy explore as much as you would a larger breed dog. Obviously, if you are walking around your neighborhood and encounter an aggressive dog, keep your puppy away so that he doesn't correlate dogs that he meets outside as being a threat. Also, keep in mind that you need to walk a distance that your puppy can handle so that you aren't tempted to pick your puppy up off the ground. You can let your puppy greet friendly dogs, which you can determine by asking the people walking the strange dog. If they say it is all right, your wee friend will get a chance to sniff noses and see that other dogs are great to meet.

Why Genetics Matter

Photo Courtesy Of Jodie Trevett

Genetics is a primary factor in how your puppy's personality develops. As a designer breed, there are far more variables than with other types of dogs since Miniature Goldendoodles' parents are two different breeds with different personality traits. Each individual puppy and each litter can be quite different, which means you can never be sure exactly what your puppy's personality will be. Though each puppy will have personality traits from both of the parents, it is far more difficult to tell which traits your puppy will inherit. Knowing the parents' personalities will help you plan for training, even though they are different breeds. If one parent tends to be shy or active, you can plan to play to the strengths and weaknesses noted by the breeder.

Overcoming Shyness

Miniature Goldendoodles aren't known for being shy, but that doesn't mean that your puppy definitely won't be. Perhaps your sidekick will be shy in the beginning, and socialization will help overcome that initial shyness. Let the puppy initiate interactions so that your new family member doesn't feel powerless. The whole family will need to sit away from the puppy, letting the little pup decide who to sniff and play with. This lets your puppy get familiar with the family in a way that is comfortable to him, and not forced.

Make sure that everyone remains calm and gentle during this interaction. Children need to understand how to behave and that they need to be calm during the interaction. If your child or children are being boisterous, they will need to play somewhere else while the puppy is getting to know people. It is best to keep excited children away from puppies since those children cannot control themselves and let the puppy initiate any contact.

Likewise, socialization with other dogs should be conducted in a calm, controlled environment with dogs that are naturally friendly and calm. This will help the puppy understand how to interact with dogs as much as realizing that other dogs aren't scary. With a world full of creatures that are much larger than your pooch, things can quickly get overwhelming. Calm, controlled interactions teach puppies that they don't need to be intimidated. In addition to being mellower, adult dogs can also help be a positive influence in getting your puppy to be calmer.

Photo Courtesy Of
Sarah Jones

Common Problems

The Miniature Goldendoodle is not a dog that tends to have personality problems or bad behavior. They are inclined toward being playful and having a great time with people, and their typical personality traits are best described as positive and affable. They tend to be gentle, patient, loyal, and companionable. However, lack of socialization could result in problems not typically associated with the breed, with small dog syndrome being the most significant problem.

Properly Greeting New People

That adorable little puppy is going to look like a cuddly stuffed animal to other people (and probably to you for several months), and that means that people are going to want to greet your new family member. It is possible that some people will not understand proper etiquette and will try to pick up your bundle of fur. People who act without getting approval first should be avoided if they don't listen when you explain that your puppy should not be held.

The same rules apply out of the house as inside—let your puppy initiate the interaction. Strangers can get low and hold out a hand, but the little dog should approach them, not the other way around. You want the experience to be fun and exciting for your young friend. This means things should be on the puppy's terms so that they don't feel like they are being overwhelmed. By initiating contact, the puppy will develop a sense of comfort when he is outside of the home.

Behavior Around Other Dogs

Since this breed loves pretty much everyone and everything, early socialization should be enough to help get them on the way to be the wonderful dogs they have the potential to be. Neglecting to socialize the puppy, being overprotective of the puppy, or allowing him to do things that you would not want an adult dog to do will increase the odds that your dog will have behavior problems.

Keep the first puppy meetings with other dogs to dogs you already know. The dogs should always be proven to be friendly and easygoing. Having interactions in a controlled and friendly environment will help your puppy feel safe with other dogs so that he can grow into a happy, playful adult.

CHAPTER 10
Being A Puppy Parent

Photo Courtesy Of
Kristin Piltz

Having a puppy can be both exhilarating and exhausting. They have boundless amounts of energy for bursts of time, and then they pass out for hours. From that energy swing to the completely different take on their surroundings, puppies can make us rethink our view of the world. This new perspective comes with a lot of work. Since the puppy has everything to learn, you are going to have to expect there will be messes to clean up and some destruction to minimize. When your Miniature Goldendoodle is a puppy, there will be a lot of fun and frustration as the puppy learns the ropes.

Bonding is almost certainly going to be an easy task because this is a breed that loves to be with others. They will want to get to know the people in their new home, so as long as you provide the right environment, it will be a much faster (and incredibly rewarding) process. They will quickly learn how to pick up on your emotions and reactions to them, and they will work to get those positive responses. If you feel nervous about something, your puppy is going to notice and will also react. That cute little face will probably follow you everywhere around the house, and when you leave, that cutie is going to be depressed. Pretty soon, your puppy's world will probably revolve around you and your family. And your life will revolve around the puppy—imagining life without that sweet little one will be very difficult.

Staying Consistently Firm

Photo Courtesy Of
Bonnie Wendt

Having such an affable puppy will make it feel acceptable to let certain rules slip occasionally, but you really can't. Your job as a puppy parent is to be consistent with your small canine, just as it is important to be consistent with rules for your children. You have to be firm and say no to your puppy when rules are broken so that he learns that you are serious. Nor can you allow there to be any exceptions because your Miniature Goldendoodle will start to figure out what happened to allow that exception and will try to replicate it. All it will take is trying it again later, and soon enough, you will be wrapped around your puppy's paw, and there will be no way to take back control.

Training your wee pup requires consistency. All intelligent dogs need to see that their people are serious and that rules always apply and that lets them be the fantastic dogs they have the potential to be. Being firm is the best way to make sure your puppy reaches his full potential.

It is going to be far more difficult to be firm because it is easy to feel that letting the bad behavior go once or twice is fine. After a long day, you are going to want to relax, and enforcing the rules is going to be one of the last things you want to do. This is why planning ahead is important. You will need to mentally prepare yourself to enforce the rules at all times. Fortunately, your puppy is going to respond very well to positive reinforcement, even without food. Keeping a cool head and spending time playing with your small buddy for following the rules will be incredibly effective in getting your puppy to learn how to behave. In the end, being consistent and firm while staying calm will help your pup develop into a fantastic, loving companion.

Photo Courtesy Of
Anna Scott Lewis

Possible Problems With Miniature Goldendoodles

The biggest potential problem with this breed is small dog syndrome. Given how cute and lovable they are, you are more likely to want to protect them and treat them in a different way than you treat larger breeds. You really need to let your puppy learn and figure things out the way you would allow a larger puppy to learn. Do not encourage the idea that the world is a place to fear, and you don't want them to think that they need to intimidate other dogs. This is an undesirable quality for canines, and is something you should start to train your dog to avoid from those early days.

Given the fact that your puppy is part Retriever, it is possible that there may be an interest in chasing small animals. Train your puppy to ignore them so that they don't pull on your arm or shoulder. If your dog grows up to be on the larger side of the breed, pulling will be a lot harder to control than it is with those dogs that weigh only 15 pounds. Regardless of size, you don't want your dog to chase any animal into a street.

Photo Courtesy Of
Kelly Sayers

Playtime!

HELPFUL TIP
Intelligent Dogs
Can Find Trouble

Both Golden Retrievers and Toy Poodles are very intelligent dog breeds. Without enough physical and mental exercise to keep their brains busy, they will find creative ways to get into trouble, like figuring out how to nudge a chair or box over to a counter to reach something tasty.

Easily one of the best things about having a Miniature Goldendoodle, playtime is so much fun and there is so much potential. Your puppy is going to want to play with you as long as you are willing to play, and will generally enjoy being with you even if you aren't playing. After a short training session, your newest family member will be happy to play or just chill based on what you want to do. Playing will be fun too because your little guy is smart. The manner of play can change from day to day because your puppy is going to be able to learn new games relatively quickly.

You will find that your pooch will be less pleased by spending time alone. Leaving a Miniature Goldendoodle home alone for a few hours will be difficult on the puppy, so make sure that you save time to play as soon as you return home. This provides reassurance to your little companion.

Regular playtime should be a normal part of your schedule, and that can include the time you spend on training. As long as you are enforcing the rules, playing and training can overlap, especially if your puppy takes after the Retriever side of its genetics. Remember that puppies cannot train for too long. Your young dog requires short sessions from those earliest days, and the sessions should focus on the basics. Over time, you can add other tricks and lengthen the training sessions.

CHAPTER 11
Living With Other Dogs

Given how friendly the breed is, you aren't likely to encounter a lot of issues introducing your Miniature Goldendoodle puppy to any of the other dogs already in your home (at least not from the puppy's side). They may be a bit frisky and could decide to eat some of your clothing if you are not careful, but you can discourage this in the early days. However, they aren't likely to be territorial or aggressive. They aren't fans of being alone, and having another dog or other dogs around can actually be a real help as your young pup gets a little older and is allowed to spend time out of the puppy area when you aren't home.

First, you have to get the new puppy accustomed to the other dogs, and vice versa. Getting them familiar with each other is essential, and the approach you take to it will vary based on how your other dogs feel about the new addition. Typically, you aren't going to have to worry too much about the puppy, unless you have an older dog who is cranky, in which case the older dog won't be likely to be a fan of the new family member and all of that energy that he has. Regardless of your other dog's disposition, you are going to need to give all canine parties time to get to know each other before you leave them together without supervision. There are high odds that your puppy is going to be just fine doing whatever your other dogs do, so he isn't going to be focused on trying to be the alpha dog.

Photo Courtesy Of
Sarah Jones

Introducing Your New Puppy

The puppy should always be introduced on neutral ground, even if your dog or dogs are friendly. You are about to make a huge change to their world, so you want everyone to be on relatively even footing during that first meeting. Your dogs will be more at ease meeting a puppy when he is not in their territory, and the puppy will have more room to romp and explore the other dog or dogs while they are all comfortable with one another.

As your dog feels more comfortable with the little guy in this neutral territory, you can start preparing to head home. Once you get there, the pack mentality will already start to have a little effect because the dog and puppy were in the car together. You will still need to keep your puppy secluded when there aren't any adults around to supervise the canine interactions. If you have children, make sure they understand that the puppy is not to be

HELPFUL TIP
Friendliness

Golden Retrievers are typically very friendly with other dogs, while Toy Poodles may be more standoffish, so it's hard to predict how your Miniature Goldendoodle will react to other dogs in your home. The key is to take socialization slowly and watch for cues that either dog is uncomfortable.

played with unless there is an adult around to supervise this interaction as well. The combination of child, puppy, and dog can be bad if there isn't an adult around to keep the interactions calm. The designated puppy space will make the dog feel better because there will be time away from the puppy. The new little buddy will be happy because there will be a place to go to just relax after all of the stimulation. This is why it is absolutely essential to have the puppy area set up and secured before he arrives.

There shouldn't be anything in the puppy area that belongs to any of the other dogs, cats, or other animals. Having toys or other items belonging to the other pets in the puppy area is problematic because it creates unnecessary tension between the puppy and your dog. Although Miniature Goldendoodles don't tend to be destructive, all puppies chew on items around them. To keep the little one from destroying your other dog's stuff, keep it out of the puppy area. If the puppy does get to your other dog's toys, this could be seen by your dog as a challenge to the established pack hierarchy. To keep your dog from feeling threatened, the puppy should not be able to interact with any non-puppy toys or items (including dog food and bedding).

Feeding time should be done in different locations. Food is one thing that nearly every breed will be protective of, so avoid unnecessary aggression by keeping the canines separated during feeding time. As time passes, the puppy and the dog can start moving closer together during mealtime, but in the early days, keep eating areas in different locations. You need to plan for this prior to the new canine's arrival; know where the puppy will eat, but don't change the older dog's normal eating location.

One of the most important things to do before the puppy arrives is to make sure your schedule includes daily playtime with your current dog or dogs. They will need designated playtime with you to reassure them that you still care about them since you are going to be spending a considerable amount of time with the new little guy. It is very likely your older dog will be nervous with the new addition, or will experience some level of new stress, and the one-on-one time with you helps them relax. Be prepared for a bit of jealousy when your dog realizes that the puppy is a permanent addition to the family. For example, your new canine's training time should not take place when you usually go for a walk with your current dog. The designated puppy training and playtime need to be intentionally during times when you aren't usually spending time with your original dog.

You are going to need to be even stricter about the rules with another dog. If you don't let your dog on the couch, you can never let the puppy on the couch either. Letting the new guy break the rules not only teaches your newest addition the wrong lesson, it can create resentment since your dog doesn't have the same option to cuddle with you on the couch.

As long as you treat the puppy and the dog the same way and with the same rules, you stand to gain a lot from the positive relationship you are fostering. Older dogs can teach the new puppy the ropes, acting as a bit of a babysitter or authority when the people aren't around. This in-

cludes helping during the training. If your dog knows how to do tricks that you want your puppy to do, you have a built-in assistant to demonstrate the right reaction to commands. Your older dog is also very likely to enforce the rules too, as long as you have been consistent (if you haven't been, be prepared for your dog to rebel and do the same stuff as the puppy, which means retraining your older dog while trying to train the new one). Since your original dog is more likely to be immune from giving in to that cute cuddly appearance than people are, you can count on the dog to provide the right guidance.

Of course, if your dog has no desire to help train (which is likely for elderly dogs), don't force them. It is perfectly fine for your dog to take a more paws off approach to the puppy—your dog didn't bring that little creature home and is not responsible for his behavior. Let the dog and the puppy establish a natural relationship that makes both of them comfortable to keep your home a peaceful place.

Playful Dog Mentality

Playtime is rarely going to feel like a chore with a Miniature Goldendoodle. They are going to want to play all of the time, and that is probably going to cheer you up, even after a long work day. That enthusiasm and positivity are contagious, which is a part of what makes this such a popular breed. Playing is a lot more fun than training; however, all of the existing rules must still apply during playtime. You can't break the rules even when you are playing with your puppy and dog. If you let that pitiful puppy-eyed stare sway you

Photo Courtesy Of Joyce Hughes

once, you are going to be facing chaos from all your canine companions in no time. Your Miniature Goldendoodle will be able to figure out pretty quickly what caused you to break the rules, and the expectation will be that the action will work in the future. Having a sweet little face constantly pushing the boundaries is one problem, but if your dog figures it out too (or worse, first), you are going to find it nearly impossible to go back to applying the rules.

You will need to let the puppy and your dog have time to interact with supervision. The older your puppy gets, the more stamina the small canine will develop. This will probably be very welcome to your other dogs because it means another playmate for regular activities. Make sure that they have ample time to play outside, even if they don't play out there at the same time. Over time, you can play with both your older dog and a more mature puppy at the same time, so help them get there a little faster.

Biting, Fighting, and Puppy Anger Management

As a fun-loving and affable dog, the Miniature Goldendoodle is not known for being aggressive or biting. But all puppies have to learn not to bite, and those little teeth are sharp. It is something you need to plan to train your puppy not to do. Like all other training, you are going to need to be calm and level-headed while you are training them not to bite. Admittedly, this can be difficult when it hurts, but you need to mentally prepare yourself to deal with it calmly to help the puppy train out of it faster. They don't know not to do it, so you need to be patient during training. Remain firm and consistent during training, and remember that positive reinforcement goes a long way with this breed.

You will also need to make sure that your pup doesn't develop small dog syndrome; do this by treating the puppy like a dog instead of spoiling the little guy. Sure, they are adorable, but they aren't as fragile as they look. Be careful with them, but not overprotective. Let the puppy learn to socialize with other dogs and people early on, and you probably aren't going to have problems with this.

Raising Multiple Puppies at Once

Raising multiple puppies at the same time is a unique challenge. It is all of the chores, training, and frustration multiplied by the number of puppies. While they can learn from each other, they can also undermine you together. Choosing to raise more than one Miniature Goldendoodle will take a considerable amount of work, although you are fortunate in that they will learn fairly quickly and can reinforce what they have learned with each other.

Consistency is a must with multiple puppies, especially intelligent ones. You can allow no exceptions to the rules because it will undermine your authority. The first few weeks will be rough, and you are going to want to spend a lot more time playing than training. However, you will start to see results a lot faster if you spend time training your puppies. Once the rules are established, and the puppies understand that you are serious about those rules, training will get a lot easier. You still need to be consistent, but your wee pups are less likely to try to outsmart you or push the boundaries. They just need to know that the established boundaries are not going to move.

Your personal life is going to be nearly nonexistent during this time. Taking care of your puppies is going to consume most to all of your time. This approach is necessary so that your puppies learn to behave. You need to train them together and separately. Yes, that does mean considerably more training sessions. Since the puppies are individuals, they need time alone with you as individuals, as well as together as part of the pack.

The individual time has the added benefit of helping you better understand each puppy's unique personality as it develops. Knowing those quirks can help you to tailor training to each puppy's strengths, and they can start to teach each other the different things they know as they grow. You also need to establish bonds with each puppy, which you cannot do if you treat them as a single unit instead of as individuals. While you are training one puppy, someone will need to play with the other little guy to minimize jealousy. Even if this isn't a breed prone to jealousy, you don't want to encourage your puppies to feel left out.

When you train them together, you are going to need to minimize the amount of goofing off and distractions the puppies make. To do this, you need to remove all of your own distractions. You aren't going to be able to get the puppies to focus if you keep staring at your phone or talking to someone not participating in the training session. This is just as true when you aren't training. When you prepare their food, focus on that single task, no phone or other distractions keeping you from getting it done as soon as possible. You definitely do not want to have any distractions while you are leashing and taking your puppies for a walk— once the leashes are out, get the puppies out the door as soon as possible. They are watching you and learning. If they are excited because you brought the leashes out, then suddenly have to wait while you text a response to someone or walk back to use the bathroom, you will have two very excited puppies with no outlet apart from each other. It's not a great scenario, but it is incredibly easy to avoid by always remaining focused yourself. If you have other pets, they are not going to be pleased that you riled up the puppies with the promise of a walk, then left them full of excitement with nothing else to do. Those puppies will very likely start pouncing on other pets, which is really unfair to your older pets.

Friendly as they are, even Miniature Goldendoodle puppies can end up fighting from time to time. It could just be wrestling or some other harmless type of struggle, but you want to keep an eye on them to make sure that anything that sounds aggressive is just play. Early on, the puppies may want to establish their own hierarchy, although this is a breed that is more likely to figure out where they fit instead of forcing themselves into a certain place in the pack. If they do end up struggling over who is dominant, you will need to monitor it to ensure they don't do any real harm while they work it out.

Your puppies' reactions are essentially a reflection of your training. If you are consistent and firm with your pups, training will get easier. If you are inconsistent or distracted, your puppies will take advantage of that.

CHAPTER 12
Training Your Miniature Goldendoodle Puppy

Miniature Goldendoodles are a small to medium-sized dog with the ability to think and learn with relative ease. They aren't as intelligent as breeds like the German Shepherd or Border Collie, but they are fast learners and put those brains to good use. This is both a great trait and a reason to be careful with your puppy's training. All intelligent dogs tend to learn quickly, but that does not mean that they will always put what they learn to good use.

During all of the time they spend with you, they are learning, so you must be careful about your actions as long as your puppy is watching. Always keep that in mind.

A Gentle, Consistent Approach

Photo Courtesy Of Lucy Ciprian

A gentle, consistent approach to training your Miniature Goldendoodle ensures that the training is successful. Their fun-loving, happy disposition makes them easy to influence through positive reinforcement. They really love a positive reaction from you, and they will be very aware of what they did to get that reaction.

Being firm and consistent will be a real challenge because the Miniature Goldendoodle is so charming you are going to want to give in to them. After a long day at work or school, sitting back and relaxing is going to be what you want to do, and your Miniature Goldendoodle is going to encourage that. As tempting as it is, you can't do it. No matter how difficult your day is or how cute your puppy is, you have to take the time to train your little love. It doesn't have to be a terribly long session, but daily training is required, even if it is for just 10 to 15 minutes. Keeping to rules and schedules is incredibly important in those early days after your new friend comes home.

Training teaches your little pooch how to behave, not just how to do tricks. It is also about learning where the puppy fits into the family. After your pup learns and adjusts to the new life with your family, you can be a bit more flexible, but you have a ways to go before you can do that.

For most of the first year, be prepared to make training a daily occurrence. You are a teacher at nearly every point when you are around the puppy. This is how your new little companion is going to learn about how he is expected to fit into the pack and what the expectations are. Even if you have a mellow puppy, there is still a role for him to play in the pack. This is part of canine socialization and it is something you must keep in mind while training your little guy, particularly to keep him from developing small dog syndrome.

Gain Their Respect Early

All dogs of all breeds interact with other dogs and people based on a level of respect they have for others. Without respect, your dog will be less enjoyable to be around and will take advantage of the position he perceives he is in for your pack, and he is less likely to listen to you. Hierarchies are a primary component of dog socialization.

You don't need to teach your puppy to fear you, though; rather, you must take a consistent, firm approach to interacting with your dog. There is a big difference between respect and fear. Fear is entirely unnecessary with a breed like the Miniature Goldendoodle. The puppy's desire to have fun with you and to make you happy is more than enough to motivate your new family member. Being consistent and firm with your puppy is all that it takes to encourage him to learn and act the way you want him to. He will also be a lot more comfortable as he learns what the rules are. By knowing how he fits into the pack, he will be happy.

Developing a strong bond with your doggy is critical, and easy to do with positive reinforcement. When your puppy responds to you the way you want him to, love and affection are ample for encouraging that behavior in the future. Treats can work, but it isn't any more effective than positive interactions. The time spent training is time when you and the pooch are bonding. Your Miniature Goldendoodle mostly wants to spend time with you. As your small canine learns what behaviors get positive responses, the rules will be more obvious, and that will make training easier as this starts to click in your puppy's mind.

Operant Conditioning Basics

Operant conditioning is simply the scientific term for actions and consequences. This is exactly what your Miniature Goldendoodle needs to learn—how certain actions gain positive consequences.

Since this is a friendly, affable breed, positive reinforcement works wonders. Smarter dogs know that a happy human is more enjoyable to be around, and Miniature Goldendoodles will also crave the praise that comes with the right actions. Hearing that they have done well goes a lot further to encourage the behavior you want than using negative reinforcement.

There are two types of reinforcements for operant conditioning;

- Primary reinforcements
- Secondary reinforcements

You will use both during your Miniature Goldendoodle training.

*Photo Courtesy Of
Tracy Helmer*

Primary Reinforcements

A primary reinforcement gives your dog something that it needs to survive, with food being one of the most common reinforcements. However, positive social interaction is another primary reinforcement type, and the one you should opt to use more often. Miniature Goldendoodles love to be with you, so hearing praise from you is highly effective during training.

Initially, you may want to rely on primary reinforcements because your young Miniature Goldendoodle will not need training to enjoy them. Food is generally something that is wonderful to have outside of mealtime, and extra time and attention from you is always welcome. However, do be careful about striking a balance with food as a reward. Mealtime and playtime should never be denied to your Miniature Goldendoodle, no matter how poorly the pup performed during training. These are essentials to living, so you have to provide them—that is not negotiable. It is the extra treats and playtime that are up for negotiation and what you use to reinforce good behavior.

Always err on the side of providing too much attention and affection, while being relatively stingy on the treats. Your Miniature Goldendoodle is not going to get very big, and you do not want the puppy to learn to overeat.

Secondary Reinforcements

When you take up a new hobby or physical activity, you do a lot of repetition to improve. The improvement that comes with repetition is secondary reinforcement. Pavlov's experiment with dogs is probably the most widely known example. Pavlov tested dogs, teaching them to associate the ringing of a bell with mealtime. They were conditioned to associate the bell with a primary reinforcement—food. The same thing is true with cats and can openers; they may come to associate the sound with food and come running toward the kitchen when they hear it.

Secondary reinforcements work very well with Miniature Goldendoodle because your puppy will associate the trigger with something that is required. This reinforces that particular behavior. Dogs that are taught to sit using a treat only will automatically react by sitting when you offer a treat, even if you don't tell them to. They know that the treat in your hand means that they should sit. Of course, this is not the type of training you want to reinforce because you want your Miniature Goldendoodle to sit on command, not when you have food in your hand. This is

HELPFUL TIP

Easier Training Than Other Breeds

Both Golden Retrievers and Toy Poodles are very intelligent dog breeds. Without enough physical and mental exercise to keep their brains busy, they will find creative ways to get into trouble, like figuring out how to nudge a chair or box over to a counter to reach something tasty.

why it can be tricky to move to secondary reinforcers.

Fortunately, you have the advantage with Miniature Goldendoodles when you use praise as a reward. They do enjoy extra food, but not nearly as much as they enjoy your attention and positive interaction.

Toys can also be used to get your puppy to act the right way. If you have a regular schedule that you can adjust to give your Miniature Goldendoodle a little extra attention for doing really well, that is just as effective, if not more so, for this particular breed.

Sometimes punishment is required, but it really should be used sparingly. When your Miniature Goldendoodle does something you don't like or that it shouldn't do, ignoring your family member is far harsher than any other kind of punishment because the puppy craves interaction. All you need to do is put the little dog back in the designated puppy area and walk away, but not out of sight. No matter how much your small friend whimpers, just ignore the behavior, no matter how much you want to give in. This reinforces that you are not happy with his behavior.

To reinforce behavior, the reward or punishment must be almost immediate. With too much time between the misbehavior and the punishment, your puppy is not going to understand why the punishment has occurred, and could associate the wrong action with the punishment.

If the pooch whines and whimpers to let you know that it is time to go outside and you fail to act, that is not the puppy's fault, so you should not be punishing your Miniature Goldendoodle. You have to learn the puppy's signals as much as he needs to learn your instructions.

When praising or punishing your Miniature Goldendoodle, keep eye contact during all of it. This may require holding the scruff of your puppy's neck gently to force him to look into your eyes (obviously only for punishment as your puppy will look you in the eyes and wag that little tail for praise).

Why Food Is A Bad Reinforcement Tool

Food is always a flawed reward. Even if your puppy matures into a medium-sized dog, treats should be used sparingly after the early days. With a companionable breed like the Miniature Goldendoodle, you can transition to mostly positive interactions fairly early because it is just as effective as food. Treats should primarily be used when you are short on time or when it is late and you need to get to bed (the housetraining is going to be rough, so treats will be your best option—you probably won't be awake enough to really interact with your little guy). Otherwise, it is best to stick to giving him positive attention instead of using food as an incentive.

Treats are probably a better incentive in the early days because the puppy is growing and has a quick metabolism. They will also have a good bit of energy, so they can burn off the calories fairly quickly. While the puppy learns how to react to commands, treats provide a more immediate reward. Treats are easier to understand until he understands how to interact with you. It will be easier for your puppy to understand to follow treats for commands like "come" or "roll over" too. You can lead them with the treat, and then hand it over when they successfully follow the treat.

The three commands that will require treats are "sit," "stay," and "leave it." These words won't mean anything to your small dog initially, and the treat bridges the meaning of the command with the puppy's re-action to it. The command "leave it" will probably be the most difficult for him to learn, especially with the Retriever heritage, and treats give him a reason to let go of whatever you want dropped.

Small Steps To Success

The first few weeks and months that you are together with your Miniature Goldendoodle are going to be rough, and they will feel very long because your puppy has had little to no training, meaning everything must be learned from the very beginning. This is going to be most obvious with housetraining. You will need to start slowly and build up the daily routine. Being in a new home, with all of the new people and sounds, is going to be both exciting and scary for the puppy. That first week or two will pose a lot of distractions for him. As your Miniature Goldendoodle becomes acclimated to the new environment, boredom may set in, making training more effective.

Photo Courtesy Of
Roxanne Kellen

Despite the distractions, you should start the training as soon as your puppy arrives; it will just be in small steps. This plants the seed in your pooch's mind about what training is. During this time you can also begin crate training because it provides a safe place that is familiar and is just for your new family member. At some point, your Miniature Goldendoodle may not need the crate anymore, especially if you allow him to sleep on the bed or couch, but it is a nice, safe place for your puppy in those early days.

Why Trainers Aren't Always Necessary

Because they are so companionable, you should be able to train your Miniature Goldendoodle puppy without assistance. It is a great opportunity to bond, so as long as you can dedicate the time needed to complete the basic training, you won't need a trainer. Your puppy will be more interested in being with you than interacting with a stranger for these lessons. It will also be less effective as your puppy will learn to listen to someone else instead of you.

As long as you can be patient and positive with your little friend, as well as remaining firm and consistent, you shouldn't need help training your little pup to follow the commands in the next chapter. Their intellect will also speed up the process, and they will crave the attention and activity that comes with training.

CHAPTER 13
Basic Commands

With the parentage of this fantastic, affable breed, you know that you are very likely going to get an intelligent dog that understands what you want pretty quickly. You will have years of being able to teach all kinds of fun tricks that your dog will be more than happy to learn. Commands like roll over, high five, and play dead may take a little more time to teach, but your dog can learn them and will love to show off in front of everyone. Fetch will probably be surprisingly easy for your Miniature Goldendoodle to learn, so if you like to play Frisbee or ball, your dog will be absolutely delighted to play with you.

Why Size And Personality Make Them Ideal Companions

Miniature Goldendoodles tend to be an amazing dog, but they still require training. You don't have to go overboard and teach them a wealth of tricks, but they should at least know the basics so that they will listen to you. Getting them to learn the basic commands in this chapter will make them responsive to you for the necessary commands, which also will provide some protection from themselves. You can keep them from running out in the road or eating something dangerous if you teach them stay and leave it. The other commands are incredibly useful and help to calm them down when they get too excited, particularly sit. Leave it is easily the best command in this chapter for you to teach your pup because your Miniature Goldendoodle may try to eat questionable items, and this command will make your dog instantly drop whatever he or she is trying to eat. It is also the most difficult command for your pup to learn as it goes against the dog's nature. For training, you will be getting your Miniature Goldendoodle to drop a toy or other item for a treat, which will go more smoothly than you think. Fetch is in the Retriever blood, so even if it takes longer to teach than the other commands, it will be much easier to teach it to your puppy than it takes for most other breeds.

Picking The Right Reward

For this particular breed, the right reward will vary based on where you are in the training. In the beginning, treats will be the best incentive, but it won't take too long before petting and affection will start to work too. You will want to make the switch as early as possible, though you will likely use both for most of the training.

Petting and play are highly effective as rewards once your puppy understands the point of training. As your little guy starts to respect you, you can begin to use more petting as a great incentive to get him to follow the commands consistently. Of course, when you start training there won't be any respect because that will take a little while to build. By the time you reach the command leave it though, your puppy will have learned to respect you. While you will definitely need to use treats for this order, also petting your little trainee will help to get the point of the command across that much faster.

When you finish a training session, give your puppy extra attention and love, maybe by giving some extra belly rubs or playing with a toy or two. This will help make the puppy excited for the next training session.

Photo Courtesy Of
Jillian Wise

Successful Training

Training focuses on your puppy learning different commands. If your young trainee learns to respond to the treat and not the commands, the training was not successful.

The reason that dogs learn the commands is because they develop a respect for their people. As you work with your little canine, you are both bonding and teaching your puppy to respect you (keeping in mind respect comes from a consistent, firm approach during training). Give your puppy time to learn to respect you, because wanting to play with you and learning to follow commands are very different ideas. You can use the desire to play to help coax your doggy into respect though, and if you are consistent and calm during training, this sends the right messages to your puppy. Once you have the puppy's respect, you can start using positive actions (not just treats) to motivate your young companion to listen.

Even if positive attention doesn't work as a suitable reward quite yet during training, you should include it. Over time, your puppy will understand that positive attention correlates to the desired behavior. Once this becomes clear to your puppy, training should get easier. Associating the extra attention and petting as a reward encourages your pup to look at playtime as a great reward. Even if your Miniature Goldendoodle loves food, playing and attention are just as enjoyable, and maybe even a bit more so.

HELPFUL TIP

Why "Drop It" and "Leave It" Are Crucial Commands

Sure, videos of people chasing their dog around, trying to get it to drop something, are adorable, but getting your dog to drop something toxic without a fuss could save his life—and getting your dog to avoid rolling in something dead with a "leave it" command might save your nose!

Basic Commands

All puppies should learn five basic commands. After learning these commands, your Miniature Goldendoodle will have all of the necessary foundations to understand what training is and that there is always something to learn during that time. Then you can start teaching your puppy the more exciting tricks.

Follow the list in the order provided. Sit is considered the most basic command, and it is something that your Miniature Goldendoodle already does naturally. That makes it easier for the puppy to understand what you want. Leave it is the most difficult command, so you will need to build up your puppy's understanding of training. Dropping something is not a natural reaction for your dog, especially if the puppy has food in his mouth, so you are working against instinct with this one. It will take longer to train for this command, so have the necessary tools already in place to improve your chance of successfully teaching this order.

The following are basic guidelines for training.

- Everyone in the home should be part of the training session because your Miniature Goldendoodle needs to learn to listen to everyone in the family.
- Have a designated training area and make sure there are no distractions for you or the puppy. Leave your phone and other mobile devices out of sight so that your attention is given completely to the puppy and training.
- Stay positive and excited about the training. Your Miniature Goldendoodle puppy is going to pick up on your emotions, so if you are enthusiastic, your puppy will be too.
- Be consistent as you teach.
- Bring a special treat to the first few training sessions, like cheese or small pieces of meat.

Sit

After settling in with the special treat, start training. Sit will be relatively easy. Wait until your puppy starts to sit down, and say sit before the motion is done. If your puppy finishes sitting, give praise and a little bit of treat. Naturally, this will make your puppy excited and wiggly, so you may need to wait for the excitement to settle before you try again. When your puppy calms down and starts to sit, repeat the process.

This will take several sessions, probably even a couple of weeks, for the puppy to really understand the concept. Miniature Goldendoodles are smart, but following commands is an entirely new idea. However, once your young friend understands the purpose and how to react to the command, the puppy's brain will be working to connect your next command with the appropriate action.

Wait until your puppy can consistently follow your instructions before moving on to the next command.

Down

Follow the same process for down. When the puppy starts to lie down, say down. If the Miniature Goldendoodle finishes the action, offer the reward. This will probably take less time once you start training. Once your puppy demonstrates a mastery over the command, you can move on to the next command.

Photo Courtesy Of
Michelle Geshrick

Stay

This command will be more difficult to teach since your Miniature Goldendoodle is going to want to follow you everywhere. Be prepared for this order to take at least twice as long to teach as sit because this is entirely counter to your puppy's nature and desire. It is also important that your pup has mastered both of the other commands first.

Choose whether you want your puppy to be sitting or lying down when you tell the puppy to stay. You will need to start with the puppy in this position for the rest of the training sessions until your Miniature Goldendoodle has mastered the command.

Tell your puppy to stay from either a sitting or lying position. When you do, place your hand in front of the puppy's face. Wait until the puppy stops trying to lick your hand before you begin again.

When the puppy settles down, take a single step away. If your puppy does not move, say stay and offer a treat along with some praise.

The reward indicates that the command is over, but you need to signal that it is also complete by repeating the command. The puppy must learn to stay until you indicate that it is okay to leave. Once you give the okay, do not offer any more treats. Come should not be used as your okay word as it is another basic command.

Repeat these steps, taking more steps away from the puppy as he shows the ability to stay.

Once your puppy understands this command, start training to stay even if you are not moving. Extend the amount of time required for the puppy to remain in one place so that he understands that stay ends with the okay command.

When you feel confident that your puppy has learned the command, you can move to the next command.

Come

Your puppy needs to have mastered the previous three commands before starting this one. The other two commands do not require the puppy to have experience with commands to start (it is just easier to train if the puppy already has an understanding of what commands are and how he or she should react).

Before you start with come, decide if you want to use come or come here. You and the family must be consistent in using just one of those two commands. Once you know which one to use, make sure the rest of the family knows too.

Leash your Miniature Goldendoodle.

Tell the puppy to stay and move away.

Say your chosen version of the come command and give the leash a gentle tug. As long as you did not use the term to indicate that the stay command is over, your puppy will start to understand the new command. If you used the term to indicate the end of stay, this will just confuse your puppy as your puppy associates come with a part of stay, and not as its own command.

Repeat these steps, building a larger distance between you and the puppy. When he understands the command, remove the leash, and start close again. If the puppy seems to have problems without the leash, you can provide visual clues, such as patting your lap. Your Miniature Goldendoodle will definitely want to sit in your lap. Provide the reward as soon as your puppy reaches you.

Leave It

This is going to be one of the most difficult commands you will teach your puppy because it goes against both the Miniature Goldendoodle's instincts and interests. Your puppy wants to keep whatever he or she has in the mouth, so you are going to have to offer something better. It is essential to teach this command early though, as your dog is going to be very destructive in the early days. You want to get the trigger in place to convince the puppy to drop things.

You may need to start teaching this outside of the training arena as it has a different starting point.

Start when you have time to dedicate to the lesson. You have to wait until the puppy has something in his or her mouth to drop. Toys are usually the best thing to get your dog to drop. Offer the puppy a special treat. As the pup drops the toy, say leave it, and hand over the treat.

This is going to be one of those rare times when you must use a treat because your puppy needs something convincing as a reason to drop the toy. For now, your puppy needs that incentive, something more tempting than what he or she already has to learn the command.

This will be one of the two commands that will take the longest to teach (quiet being the other one). Be prepared to be patient with your pup. Once your puppy gets it, start to teach leave it with food. This is incredibly important to do because it could save your dog's life. They are likely to lunge at things that look like food when you are out for a walk, and being so low to the ground, they are probably going to see a lot of food-like objects long before you do. This command gets them to drop whatever they are munching before ingesting it.

Where To Go From Here

Typically, Miniature Goldendoodles are relatively quick learners, which will make training that much better. Even if your puppy isn't the fastest learner, it will be enjoyable time spent together. You may find yourself just as eager to train as your little trainee is to learn. It is one of the best sources of entertainment and bonding, and there are plenty of perfect tricks for your adorable Miniature Goldendoodle to learn.

Ensure your Miniature Goldendoodle knows the commands in this chapter before you start any other training. Many of the tricks that your puppy learns will be based on one of these commands, but even for tasks that don't . The initial training is actually as much about training your puppy how to train as it is about learning the commands. When you teach these tricks first, you provide a much wider range of potential as well since there are so many tricks that require that your dog be able to do the five basic commands. Proba-

Photo Courtesy Of
Lisa McClain

bly the most fun will be fetch with your Miniature Goldendoodle, and leave it is an essential factor in getting this trick to work right. Over time, your puppy will learn to drop the toy without you having to say anything because fetch will very likely be a favorite game.

If your puppy has trouble learning these basic commands, spend extra time making sure that your puppy understands them before you try teaching him any other tricks. If you still want to train your puppy as the little guy matures, make sure that the training sessions are reasonable. You shouldn't be pushing your dog too far, too fast.

CHAPTER 14
Nutrition

Your puppy's diet is every bit as important as your own. You will need to be very careful with what you feed your Miniature Goldendoodle puppy from the beginning to ensure that the little pup doesn't get accustomed to overeating or have a steady diet of unhealthy food. What your dog eats will affect both the dog's health and energy levels.

You are in almost complete control over what your Miniature Goldendoodle eats (every dog parent knows that dogs will manage to eat something on those outdoor walks, and you can't control that beyond lunging at your pup and trying to pull the food out of his mouth). The best way to control what your little one eats is to make sure that you don't have any people food where your dog can reach it, particularly in the early days. Puppies will get into your food in a heartbeat—grown Miniature Goldendoodles aren't a whole lot better. The best way to control your dog's diet is to plan meals long before the puppy arrives. The right diet ensures your dog and you can enjoy a long, happy, fun-filled life well into the dog's later years.

Photo Courtesy Of
Liza Rieke

Why A Healthy Diet Is Important

Miniature Goldendoodles have a medium level of energy and they will be fairly active, but they will also be perfectly comfortable being a couch potato with you. Like Labs, Golden Retrievers are essentially bottomless pits and they will pretty much eat as long as there is food available. If your dog takes after this side of the family, you are going to need to be far more careful of how much food your dog eats, no matter how active your canine is. You don't want your dog to have lower life quality because he or she is too obese to play.

A well-balanced diet is essential to ensure your Miniature Goldendoodle stays healthy well into the golden years. Consider how much exercise your dog will get or has gotten over the course of the day and week. If you and your dog are going to be more sedentary, you can provide smaller portions of food (not significantly less). Make sure that the food and exercise are balanced so that you aren't overfeeding or underfeeding your dog. Just as you should be aware of your own caloric intake, you should try to keep your dog's caloric intake proportionate to the energy expended. You will also need to make sure that your canine gets adequate vitamins and nutrients, not just the appropriate number of calories.

Commercial Food

Though many dog food producers say that their food is the healthiest dog food on the market, all of them are incredibly flawed. Because it is processed food, your dog's digestive system isn't going to be able to fully digest all of the nutrition, even if all of the nutrients needed are in the food. Unfortunately, most people don't think they have adequate time in the day to make their dog's food, making processed dog food their best option. It actually isn't as time consuming as you might think though, certainly not any more time consuming than managing your own meals.

If you really do not have time to make sure that your dog's dietary needs are being met, take the time to verify the options of the food you are considering purchasing. This ensures your small companion gets the right nutrients on a daily basis. Adding a few extra foods to what you serve your dog can provide supplemental nutrients. It will also provide a new flavor that your dog will likely enjoy a lot more than just dry dog food.

Preparing Your Food Naturally At Home

Adding a little extra cooking or food preparation to your day for your dog will not actually take as much time as you may think. If you are careful about what you eat, it doesn't take that much more to make sure your dog gets a balanced diet either—it actually may be easier since you don't have to consider taste as much as you do for yourself. For Miniature Goldendoodles that take after the Retriever side, eating itself is a pleasure. Of course, your Miniature Goldendoodle has significantly different dietary needs than you do, but the same foods that you eat can be mixed into your dog's food if they meet your dog's dietary needs. Foods like vegetables and eggs provide fantastic supplemental nutrition and flavor to the food. Before doing this though, make sure to review the list of foods that are deadly for your canine, and do not give these foods to your dog.

You should feed your dog either while you are eating or after you are done (you don't want your dog to get accustomed to being the first one fed because this implies your dog is the alpha). While it may not be likely that your dog will think of itself as the alpha, you want to make sure to keep the lines clear. By giving your dog the same foods that you eat, you are saving time and providing a better diet. The best home-cooked meals need to be planned though. This ensures that your dog gets the right nutrition on a regular basis. Canines have the following needs:

- 50% animal protein (such as poultry, organ meats, and oily fish)
- 25% complex carbohydrates
- 25% vegetables and fruits.

Always make sure that the foods you consider are not on the list of hazardous foods for dogs. Pumpkins, apples (remove the seeds as they are poisonous to dogs), green beans, and bananas are all fantastic foods for your dog and have an appealing smell to a dog. The real benefit to these foods is that they can make your dog feel full faster than other types of fruits and vegetables.

Puppy Food Vs. People Food

Miniature Goldendoodle puppies should always have food specifically designed for puppies. Do not feed your puppy people food from your plate, because that is both a bad precedent to set and very unhealthy for your puppy. That adorable little face will be right there expecting food every time you eat, and it will only take more to retrain your puppy over time. Don't set the expectation that your food should be shared with your puppy, especially if you are eating food that is unhealthy for your dog, like pizza or hot dogs.

Photo Courtesy Of Jillian Wise

If possible, always make your dog's food. However, it is considerably more difficult to do this for puppies as their meals require a lot more planning. Those little bodies have special needs to ensure they grow healthy and strong, particularly during those critical first few months. It you can get accustomed to making food and are aware of your puppy's nutritional needs, your puppy will have a much better first year in terms of health. Once your puppy reaches adulthood, you can switch to dog food if you find that you can't keep working the preparation of the additional food into your schedule. Preparing meals for your dog too is actually a lot better on your wallet though, as well as being better for your dog.

Dieting, Exercise, And Obesity

Photo Courtesy Of Anna Scott Lewis

Unlike people, dogs don't go on diets; they should have a regular diet that doesn't change much. This doesn't mean you should always give your dog the same foods, just that the nutrition shouldn't shift significantly as it does when a human decides to diet. If you create an expectation for treats and snacks, that is a part of your dog's regular diet, and not an exception. This is one reason why you should avoid making it a habit of providing regular treats, and why you should switch to positive reinforcements as early as you can. Instead of treats and snacks, let your dog curl up with you to watch something on TV, even if it means getting down on the floor with your dog. Extra exercise and play are also great to use as rewards instead of treats.

A healthy diet and regular exercise are essential to your dog, as well as for you. It gives you a reason to get out of bed in the morning and exercise with your dog. As you keep your dog at a healthy weight, it helps you. Having a regular exercise schedule and playtime to reward your canine is cheaper too.

Warning About Overfeeding and the Right Caloric Requirement

You need to be careful about your Miniature Goldendoodle's caloric intake, especially during the transition to adulthood. They are likely to love food, and will rarely turn it down when offered more food. Overfeeding your dog is not a reward but a hazard. Keep your dog's health in mind while feeding and training him to ensure that you aren't overindulging the pup.

HELPFUL TIP

Obesity Is a Growing Problem

More than half of all dogs in the United States are overweight or obese, and pets suffer the same health consequences from obesity as humans. You should always be able to feel your Miniature Goldendoodle's ribs. Don't love your pet to an early death with too many treats or too much food.

Regularly checking your Miniature Goldendoodle's weight can help ensure you aren't overfeeding the pup. You should be able to use your own scale to monitor their weight since they are so small. Step on the scale by yourself and check your weight, then step on the scale with your Miniature Goldendoodle. Then you just need to subtract your weight from your weight with your dog. Make sure to be honest about your own weight though because you don't want to overestimate your dog's weight. Counting calories can be very time consuming (which can help you keep from giving your dog so many treats). Still, you should be aware of roughly how many calories your Miniature Goldendoodle consumes in a day.

CHAPTER 15
Grooming—Productive Bonding

Grooming is fairly easy, though you do need to be careful of your Miniature Goldendoodle's skin. Even if you are allergic to dogs, you likely won't have a problem with this breed though. Nor will you need to dedicate too much time to the task as they do not require frequent brushing or bathing, unless they get dirty. Caring for your Miniature Goldendoodle's coat is easy, and when you are doing it, your dog will love the extra attention.

There are a few other grooming tasks that you will need to do regularly. Toenails, teeth, eyes, and ears will require attention a bit more often than the dog's coat. They may or may not mind bath time, which is also kind of nice (at least if they are indifferent). Be careful not to get your dog's ears wet during the bath as wet ears can get infected fairly easily.

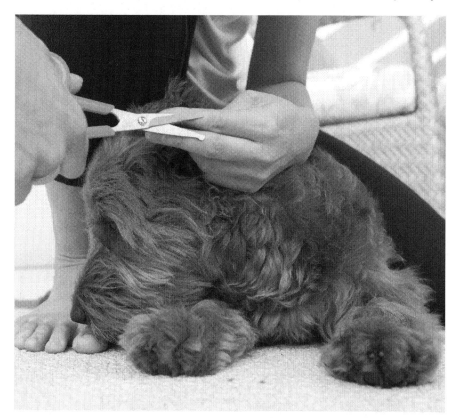

Managing Your Miniature Goldendoodle's Coat—It's Easy

While some aspects of raising a Miniature Goldendoodle can be time consuming, managing and cleaning their coats is not one of them. You can put as much time and energy into it as you want. If you want to have the fur styled like the Poodle parent's coat, you can. If you prefer a more mellow approach, that is fine too. Because it is considered to be a hypo-allergenic dog, you aren't going to have to spend nearly as much time cleaning up fur around the home.

Puppy

Brushing any puppy is usually an interesting challenge because the little guy is probably going to be incredibly wiggly and excited. Brushing will seem like playtime to him, and there is a good chance he will nip and try to knock the brush out of your hands. It will require patience and gentle coaxing to get him to stop. Although it will be cute at first, you still want to get him to stop that behavior so that you can complete the task—it will be much less cute when he is older and still thinks that brushing is playtime instead of cleaning time.

Make brushing a weekly endeavor since it will be more time consuming in the early days because of your puppy's desire to play. As your puppy learns the routine, brushing will get easier to do. To help, brush your puppy after a tiring walk when the Miniature Goldendoodle's energy is lower.

Photo Courtesy Of
Lucy Ciprian

Adulthood

Adult Miniature Goldendoodles are even easier to manage. Schedule a bath about once a quarter and occasional brushings to get out any matting that may occur, and that is about all you will need to do. Hypoallergenic dogs are preferred by many people because they don't need nearly as much care for their coats.

If you go out hiking, you may want to make time in your schedule to bathe and brush your dog afterward. The more energetic dogs will very likely be quite dirty at the end of a very active outdoor period. Though they won't require a lot of brushing and washing, you will need to keep their fur clean if you go outside a lot.

Bathing: Watch The Ears, Shampoos

Photo Courtesy OF
Bonnie Wendt

As mentioned, bathing is easy and does not need to be done often. Even though it won't be a significant burden on your schedule, you do need to be careful when you do give your dog a bath.

When you bathe your pup, make sure to inspect the ears to note if there are any infections or issues. Since Miniature Goldendoodles are a designer breed, you need to monitor them to make sure they don't have any unexpected ailments or problems (since these are unpredictable for designer dogs). Also, make sure you do not get water in their ears, checking that the ears are dry once the pup is clean. If you do get water in your dog's ears, monitor the ears for a few days to ensure they do not get infected.

Trimming The Nails

If you have not clipped a dog's nails before, it is best to let a professional take care of your pup. Puppies aren't likely to sit still long enough for you to handle the chore, and even adults aren't always the easiest to manage when it comes to something like nail clipping (particularly if they

HELPFUL TIP
Brush, Brush, Brush

Despite what many breeders would have you believe, Miniature Goldendoodle hair is very prone to matting and requires daily brushing and combing. You should be able to get a comb all the way down to the skin through every inch of your dog's fur. There's no shame in keeping your Miniature Goldendoodle 's hair short for easier maintenance.

have had a bad experience in the past with the activity). You can learn from a professional so that you can take care of your dog's nails in the future. In the beginning, you can learn how to help keep your Miniature Goldendoodle the way the professional does. When your dog responds to your calming efforts, that is when you can start working on it. You must be very careful not to cut too far into the nail. If your Miniature Goldendoodle has black nails, you need to be extra careful, or just always have the nails trimmed by a professional.

Puppies should have nails cut weekly, and adults monthly. If you walk your pup on concrete, the concrete can wear down the nails so that you can have them trimmed less frequently. Always keep an eye on the length of your canine's nails so the nails don't get too long.

Brushing Their Teeth

Though it can be a difficult grooming chore to do in the beginning, you need to take care of your Miniature Goldendoodle's teeth. Because they are puppies, this is going to be a particularly interesting task as they will be even more of a challenge when you are actually putting something in their mouth. Even as they get older, they are going to want to lick the toothpaste off of the brush.

As difficult as it is, brushing your dog's teeth keeps them from developing gum disease. It is recommended by vets to make it a daily task. You will need to get a special canine toothpaste and brush to do it.

Cleaning Ears And Eyes

Since Miniature Goldendoodles are a designer breed, it is difficult to say if ear infections are a common problem for the breed. However, it is a problem you need to watch for to keep your canine healthy. Some Miniature Goldendoodles never have any trouble with their ears, while others have chronic problems with ear infections. Then some fall somewhere in between, occasionally having trouble with ear infections. If your canine continually scratches at an ear, it is possible that the ear is infected. Hold the dog's ear up and check the color. If the inside of the ear appears to be red, that means it is infected and needs to be treated. It might also have a bit of a smell. Set up an appointment to meet the vet and get medicine to treat it. Make sure you get directions from the vet about how to treat the infection. You will also need to watch the other ear so that it doesn't get infected (if it isn't already).

The coat may be easy to care for, but you need to make sure to keep your canine's fur out of his eyes. Many Miniature Goldendoodles have a lot of hair growing around the eyes, which can become a problem later. Since you won't need to bathe them often, you will need to keep the hair around the eyes shorter to keep dirt of out of their eyes. You should also check their eyes regularly to ensure there isn't any dirt in them. Carefully clean or cut the hair around the eyes if there is dirt. If there are any tear stains, you can clean that up as well to keep dirt from accumulating,

CHAPTER 16
Basic Health Care

Miniature Goldendoodles are an incredibly easy breed to love because they are so affable. However, since they are not an established purebred, it is difficult to know what ailments they will be prone to. It is also true, though, that they are less likely to have the more common ailments for either parent breed. As long as you take good care of your dog, you are likely to have a fantastic, excited partner for a long time. Most of these are things you should already know to do, so take them as a good reminder. Other tasks are specific to the breed (as far as is possible with a designer dog), and you should make sure to add the tasks to your schedule.

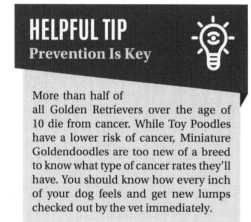

HELPFUL TIP
Prevention Is Key

More than half of all Golden Retrievers over the age of 10 die from cancer. While Toy Poodles have a lower risk of cancer, Miniature Goldendoodles are too new of a breed to know what type of cancer rates they'll have. You should know how every inch of your dog feels and get new lumps checked out by the vet immediately.

You will need to make sure to do some basic preventative care to keep your pup from suffering easily preventable problems. Most of these problems are universal to canines, not just Miniature Goldendoodles, so you can apply many of these measures for your other dogs. Come back to this chapter periodically to make sure that you remember all of the things you need to do to take proper care of your canine.

Fleas And Ticks

Miniature Goldendoodles do have sensitive skin, so flea bites can cause minor infections. You should use regular flea and tick preventative treatments to reduce problems with fleas and ticks. You may want to brush your dog a little more often in the spring and summer to keep an eye on ticks as well. During regular brushings, check your Miniature Goldendoodle for flea or tick bites, and treat any that you see.

If you take your Miniature Goldendoodle into the woods, check your canine for ticks once you are home, just like you should check yourself. This is also true if you go into a field or any area with tall grass where ticks are likely to live. You will need to comb through the Miniature Goldendoodle's longer fur, taking a close look for this parasite to make sure your dog does not have them either attached to his skin or moving up the fur. You should brush your Miniature Goldendoodle a second time within 24 hours in case you missed a tick. If you find a tick has attached itself, treat the bite.

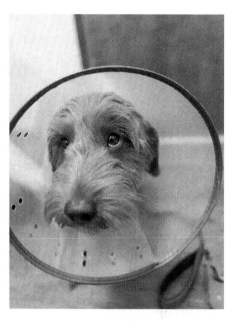

During regular brushings, keep an eye out for fleas. It will be more difficult, and it is more likely that you will see the bites instead of the fleas. That is why it is important to pay attention when you brush your Miniature Goldendoodle. If you notice your dog scratching often, take the time to check to make sure fleas are not the problem. Since Miniature Goldendoodles are a more active breed, you will likely spend more time outside, and that means being more wary of pests trying to make a home on your dog. If you regularly treat your dog and still find there is a problem with fleas, change the product you use as a part of the prevention measure.

If you would like to use a natural flea and tick preventative, research your options. You can also increase the number of baths you give your dog, but this should only be a temporary solution if your Miniature Goldendoodle is actually having a problem. Remember they do have sensitive skin, so you don't want to dry it out through frequent bathing. Make sure to verify the product's efficiency before you make any purchases for natural remedies.

Flea and tick prevention treatment should be a monthly occurrence. If you need to, set an alarm on your phone or write a reminder on your calendar to make sure you complete the treatment every month.

Worms And Parasites

Photo Courtesy Of Tracy Helmer

While these are much less of a problem, you still want to protect your little companion from them. There are many parasitic worms that could be a problem:

- Heartworms
- Hookworms
- Roundworms
- Tapeworms
- Whipworms

The following are possible symptoms that indicate that your Miniature Goldendoodle is suffering from one of these worms. If you notice any of these symptoms, schedule a visit with the vet to have your canine checked out.

- If your Miniature Goldendoodle seems unusually lethargic.
- Patches of fur begin to fall out (this will be noticeable if you brush your Miniature Goldendoodle regularly) or if you notice patchy areas in your dog's coat.
- If your Miniature Goldendoodle's stomach becomes distended (expands), set up an appointment immediately to have him or her checked. Your Miniature Goldendoodle's stomach will look like a little potbelly.
- Your dog begins coughing, vomiting, has diarrhea, or has a loss of appetite.

Many of the signs of worms can be symptoms for other problems, at least in the early stages. A visit to the vet could find that one of these parasites is the problem, or it may be something else. Whatever the problem, it is best to get your dog checked out as early as possible.

If your Miniature Goldendoodle has hookworms or roundworms, you will need to visit your doctor as well. Skin to skin contact with your Miniature Goldendoodle can pass the parasite on to you, so if your Miniature Goldendoodle has a problem, you and others in your home probably have the same problem. Everyone will need to be treated to make sure that you don't perpetuate the problem.

Heartworms are a serious problem for your Miniature Goldendoodle, and they are something you should be actively preventing for your dog. Heartworms can be deadly. There are medicines that can help your dog if the vet identifies heartworms as an issue. There are also preventative medicines to keep your dog from suffering the problem in the first place.

Benefits Of Veterinarians

You should schedule your dog for an annual visit to the vet to take care of required shots and for your Miniature Goldendoodle to get a regular checkup. Your dog requires these regular checkups just like you require at least annual visits to the doctor.

The vet visits will help detect any potential problems you may not notice. Of course, with as often as you interact with your Miniature Goldendoodle you will notice any changes in behavior. These changes in behavior could be an indication that something is wrong, in which case you should take your dog to the vet outside of the annual visit. This should not alter the regular visits though.

Health checkups are also good for ensuring that your dog is aging well. Given the fact that they are not a purebred, it can be more difficult to identify problems since it is harder to know what your dog is at greatest risk of having (unless you keep tabs on the parents and know what kinds of problems they have as they age). The vet can help you figure out ways to help you work around common canine issues such as arthritis too. They can make suggestions about things you can do to manage problems so that you don't end up spending less time with your dog. Activities like shorter walks and more indoor playtime (instead of long walks or hikes) can help keep your dog healthy and active as your Miniature Goldendoodle ages. In the end, it is worth changing the routine to keep your Miniature Goldendoodle happy and healthy well into the golden years.

Holistic Alternatives

Wanting to use a more holistic approach to caring for your Miniature Goldendoodle is understandable, but it requires considerable research before you commit to it. You do not want to take any unnecessary risks with your little companion. Unverified holistic medicines are not only a waste of time, they are a potential health risk.

Before starting use of a holistic medicine or treatment, consult your vet. You can also discuss some of the more established options with your vet rather than an untested or unverified holistic alternative. Read what scientists have had to say about each alternative. There is a chance that some of the more established treatments are better for your Miniature Goldendoodle than a holistic remedy.

Photo Courtesy Of
Bianca Barron

Vaccinating Your Miniature Goldendoodle

The vaccination schedule for your Miniature Goldendoodle is the same as it is for most dogs.

- The first shots are required at between 6 and 8 weeks following the Miniature Goldendoodle's birth. You should find out from the breeder if these have been taken care of and get the records of the shots:
  - Corona virus
  - Distemper
  - Hepatitis
  - Leptospirosis
  - Parainfluenza
  - Parvo
- These same shots are required again at between 10 and 12 weeks of age.
- These same shots are required again, along with his or her first rabies shot, at between 14 and 15 weeks old.
- Your dog will need to get these shots annually after that. Your Miniature Goldendoodle will also continue to need annual rabies shots.

Ensuring that your dog gets regular shots can help keep your newest family member happy and healthy for many years.

CHAPTER 17
Health Concerns

As with all designer breeds, it is impossible to know exactly what health issues your canine will have. Trying to guess as to what ailments a dog is likely to inherit is tricky at best. Over the few decades in which the breed has been acknowledged, several ailments have shown up more often than others. However, the best way to keep your canine healthy is to look for the ailments that are common to both of the original breeds. Since both of the parent breeds are well established (and incredibly popular in their own right), it is easier to monitor for certain common ailments. Both parent breeds are known for having several genetic maladies that you will need to watch for in your pup. This is why regular vet visits are critical—you want to catch problems as early as possible.

A Wild Card

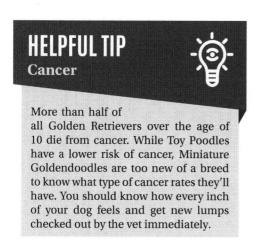

HELPFUL TIP
Cancer

More than half of all Golden Retrievers over the age of 10 die from cancer. While Toy Poodles have a lower risk of cancer, Miniature Goldendoodles are too new of a breed to know what type of cancer rates they'll have. You should know how every inch of your dog feels and get new lumps checked out by the vet immediately.

Since the Miniature Goldendoodle is not a purebred, the health concerns are not well established. Because your Miniature Goldendoodle can take on the genetics from either side, you have to learn the common health concerns for the Golden Retriever, the Miniature Poodle, and the Toy Poodle.

All designer breeds are genetic wild cards. While you must monitor them for a much wider range of potential problems, they are also less likely to have problems. The only real difference between a designer breed and a mutt is that designer breeds are bred for a particular result, which means you have a smaller pool of potential genetic issues. Like mutts, designer breeds that come from healthy parents are less likely to have the problems common to the original breeds.

Where You Can Go Wrong

Before getting into hereditary ailments, you need to know about two non-hereditary aspects that should be considered—diet and exercise. If you take good care of your dog, being careful of what your Miniature Goldendoodle eats and how often your dog exercises, the chance of some hereditary ailments is reduced. Your dog will also have a better quality of life, regardless of the genetics.

Diet

Photo Courtesy Of Lilly Hoyt

The easiest thing you can do to keep your Miniature Goldendoodle healthy is to provide the right amount of nutrients and calories for your dog's exercise level. If you have a pup that loves to be out and about, you will need to make sure that your furry baby has enough food to make it through each busy day. If your pup is mellower and prone to relaxing as much as romping, less food will be required. You will also need to keep the dog's size in mind when it comes to how much food your canine needs. Not giving your dog treats or letting him or her eat off of your plate is going to be rough in the early days, so keep in mind that you are potentially reducing your dog's lifespan by giving in to the desire to share with your new best friend.

With both parent breeds having some gastrointestinal problems (both have a history with bloat), there are plenty of reasons for you to be more careful about what you feed your Miniature Goldendoodle. If nothing else, you do not want to be cuddling up with a dog that constantly farts and vomits. You can avoid this by keeping your dog on a healthy diet.

Exercise

Photo Courtesy Of Kay Patton

Miniature Goldendoodles just want to be with you, but you can help your puppy to be healthy by making sure that there is enough exercise in every day. Given their medium energy level, it is pretty easy to ensure they have the proper activity level as long as you take them outside every day. A couple of nice walks and playing around in the house is all they really need. A solid 30 minutes of activity a day and regular training sessions are generally enough to keep them healthy if you are careful about their diet.

Many ailments are common to both breeds, including thyroid problems. If you know that your dog is getting enough exercise and is not overeating, you should probably take the pup the vet for a check should your dog start gaining weight.

Both breeds are also prone to a particular blood disease—von Willebrand disease—which increases the risk to your Miniature Goldendoodle. Making sure your dog gets exercise every day can go a long way toward reducing the risk of heart disease. However, this disease means that their blood does not clot the way it should. Pay attention to your pet for injuries. If they start to bleed and it seems to take longer than you think it should for the bleeding to stop, you may want to have the pet checked by a vet. Regular exercise is easy to do, and it is an easy way to keep your canine healthy for most of your dog's life.

Importance Of Breeder To Ensure A Healthy Miniature Goldendoodle

Knowing the health problems of the parent breeds means being able to better monitor your Miniature Goldendoodle for any of the ailments' symptoms. There are tests that should be conducted on both parent breeds. While there are no required tests for Miniature Goldendoodles, if the parents have a history of certain problems, you can have the tests conducted on your canine. It is always best to ensure that your dog is as healthy as possible, particularly when there are so many variables about their health.

If possible, find out the health and history of both parents. This is the best way to prepare for the most likely ailments your Miniature Goldendoodle may inherit. Knowing what to watch for as your dog ages can help you get the right help early enough to extend your dog's life and happiness.

Common Diseases And Conditions

Since the history of the Miniature Goldendoodle is too short for a reliable set of common risks, you should watch for the health problems that are common in both of the parent breeds.

Golden Retriever

Golden Retrievers have a few common ailments you should watch for as your dog ages, particularly if you know that one of the parents suffered from one of them. The common problems include the following:

- Canine hip dysplasia (major health problem)
- Chest conditions (major health problem common to larger breeds)
- Bloat and GDV (major/potentially deadly health problem)
- Von Willebrand disease (potentially major health problem)
- Cancer (less frequent problem)
- Loose knees (minor health problem that seriously hinders your dog's ability to play and enjoy moving—easy to treat)
- Skin conditions (minor health problem)
- Elbow dysplasia
- Eye diseases, particularly cataracts (common problem)
- Hypothyroid
- Ear infections

The ones without identifiers have varying levels of severity. All of these diseases are common in the breed, but they have significantly different levels of health concerns and not all of them are life-threatening.

Common Poodle Problems

Most of the Poodle sizes have the same health issues, so since the parent can be a Miniature or Toy Poodle, the following are the problems common for all Poodles:

- Addison's disease (major health problem)
- Bloat and GDV (major/potentially deadly health problem)
- Canine hip dysplasia (major health problem)
- Progressive Retinal Atrophy (PRA) (eye disease that could result in blindness)
- Sebaceous Adenitis (skin condition less common in Miniature and Toy Poodles)
- Luxating Patella (kneecap disease, more common in Toy Poodles)
- Legg-Calve-Perthes disease (degenerative bone disease)

Photo Courtesy Of Stefanie Stevens

- Von Willebrand disease (potentially major health problem for Miniature and Standard Poodles)
- Hyperthyroid and hypothyroid

Some of the ailments start at birth, and some breeders will test for some of the ailments on each litter. Try to find the breeders willing to run the tests to ensure your puppy is as heathy as possible. If you adopt an older dog or as your puppy ages, you will want to keep an eye on your cutie to make sure your dog is not showing symptoms of any of the health problems that are on the lists. Many of the problems are treatable with minimal health risks if caught and treated early.

Prevention & Monitoring

With genetic issues being more difficult to predict, you want to take as many preventative measures as possible. Having a regular exercise routine and healthy diet can help minimize many ailments (both hereditary and environment based). Act in your Miniature Goldendoodle's best interest. They will follow your lead, so if you are too sedentary, they will be too. If you constantly offer treats, they will eat them. Avoid these to keep your canine healthy and happy.

Monitoring your Miniature Goldendoodle for signs of ailments common in the parents can help you keep your dog's health from deteriorating as quickly as it might if the ailments go untreated. While you have a wider range of ailments to watch for, it is more than worth it. Even if your canine is less likely to suffer from common problems, it isn't guaranteed that your dog won't inherit some problems. Paying attention to your dog and setting up regular vet visits can do a lot to make sure your dog is around and active for many years to come.

CHAPTER 18
Your Aging Miniature Goldendoodle

Since the Miniature Goldendoodle is a new, designer breed, the life expectancy is not yet established. It is currently thought to be between 10 and 14 years, though this may certainly change over the decades as more data is collected. You can increase the odds of your dog living longer by taking great care of the canine, with a nutritious diet and lots of exercise. Knowing the health of the parents can also help you plan for your dog's golden years, so you can keep in contact with the breeder to stay current on how the parents are doing.

HELPFUL TIP

Vet Visits in Senior Years

Since Miniature Goldendoodles are a mix between two different breeds and are relatively new on the scene, it's hard to know what sort of health issues they may develop as they age. After your dog is about 10 years old, you should take your dog in for vet visits twice a year so the vet can catch any potential health issues before they become serious

By the time your Miniature Goldendoodle is 9, your pup will be in those golden years. The senior years can be amazing as your dog will mellow and enjoy just chilling around the home with you. It will mean making adjustments to your schedule and exercise routine, as well as to your dog's diet. A more mature dog's metabolism will slow down, so they won't require as much food (less will be better as your canine won't be able to move around nearly as much in the later years). Your sweet little pup won't be able to do all of the fun things or go on those long adventures anymore, but he or she will be more than happy to cuddle and chill with you at the end of the day.

Given the lack of established history, you will need to change your schedule to meet your dog's specific needs during the golden years. The aging process may begin very slowly, almost imperceptibly. However, your Miniature Goldendoodle is going to try to keep doing everything you want to do together because limitations are something he wants to ignore. That is why it is so important to pay attention to your Miniature Goldendoodle by the time he reaches the 8- and 9-year mark. You don't want the little pup pushing beyond the limits of aging. It is incredibly easy to accommodate your aging canine, and these years can be just as enjoyable (if a bit lazier) than the earlier years of your dog's life.

Senior Dog Care

Photo Courtesy Of Stephen Morris

It is far easier to care for an aging Miniature Goldendoodle than it is caring for a puppy. You will get more time to relax and just enjoy each other's company without worrying about your dog getting bored. If you want to sit and watch something, your Miniature Goldendoodle is perfectly happy with going out for a quick bathroom break and nestling down with you instead of taking a longer evening walk. Once your dog can't go for those long walks, include a little extra playtime in your home because your Miniature Goldendoodle should not completely forgo exercise.

Exercise and diet are just as critical during the senior years as it is for the puppy years. You can't decide that your Miniature Goldendoodle has earned all of those treats you have been denying him or her all of these years simply because the canine has reached the senior years. Since your dog isn't accustomed to frequent treats, has a slower metabolism, and can't exercise as much as needed to avoid high caloric treats, you don't want to make the last few years of your dog's life difficult by helping the pup pack on the pounds.

If you notice that your Miniature Goldendoodle is having a difficult time on longer walks, reduce the length and increase the frequency of walks. Spend more time romping around the yard or home. Your Miniature Goldendoodle will love that because it will be easy to flop down and sleep afterward—no waiting for the leash to be removed.

Be prepared to make changes around the home to accommodate your older dog. Things will be harder to reach or do as your dog's body isn't as nimble and steady as it once was. The following are some of the things you should plan to watch for and change as needed.

- Set water bowls in a few different places so that your Miniature Goldendoodle has ready, easy access to water.
- Cover hard floor surfaces (such as tiles, vinyl, and hardwood). Rugs and carpets that won't slip out from under your Miniature

Goldendoodle are important to make sure your pup doesn't get hurt just walking around the home.

- Add cushions and softer bedding for your Miniature Goldendoodle. This will make surfaces more comfortable while helping your little guy to stay warm. Remember, they do not handle cold very well, and the older they get, the easier it is for them to get cold. There are bed warmers if your Miniature Goldendoodle shows signs of achy joints or muscles.

- Increase how often you brush your Miniature Goldendoodle to improve circulation. This will help keep them a little warmer, as well as being a great way to spend time together when your Miniature Goldendoodle isn't capable of the more exciting excursions.

- Stay inside during extreme heat and cold. Your Miniature Goldendoodle may be healthy, but they aren't exactly a hardy breed when it comes to extreme temperatures.

- Use stairs or ramps instead of constantly picking your Miniature Goldendoodle up off the ground. Constantly picking your dog up may be more convenient, but it is not healthy for either you or the dog. It is best to grant your Miniature Goldendoodle as much self-sufficiency as possible during the golden years.

- Avoid remodeling and rearranging your furniture. A familiar home is far more comforting and less stressful for any aging dog.

- If your home has stairs, consider setting up an area on a single floor for your dog, and refrain from leaving that floor as much as possible. Your Miniature Goldendoodle is going to want to be wherever you are, and that includes going up and down stairs even if your dog isn't able to do it safely or without pain.

- Create a space where your Miniature Goldendoodle can relax and be alone if desired. Of course, it isn't very likely that your Miniature Goldendoodle is going to want alone time, but in case your Miniature Goldendoodle becomes a bit of a curmudgeon, a little alone space will be quite welcome when he or she isn't feeling particularly well.

- Be prepared to let your Miniature Goldendoodle out to use the restroom more often. They will not be able to hold their bladders for as long a period of time.

- Diabetes is a concern since Miniature Goldendoodles are known to develop the disease if they do not have a healthy diet. It is certainly avoidable, but it does mean making sure your Miniature Goldendoodle continues to eat healthy.

- Arthritis is a concern for dogs just as much as humans. If your dog shows signs of the ailment, such as stiffness during and pain after normal activities, it could be arthritis. You should take your pup to the vet to check and find out the best ways to help reduce the pain. Do not give your dog the same medication you take because their systems cannot handle a full pain reliever. Follow your vet's instructions, and keep medication to a minimum since these dogs are very small and their bodies cannot handle large amounts of medicine.

● Gum disease is a concern on the Poodle side. Be vigilant about brushing your Miniature Goldendoodle's teeth Also, include gum checks during regular vet visits to make sure your Miniature Goldendoodle's mouth is healthy too.

● Loss of eyesight is common in all dog breeds (as well as in humans). Unlike humans, however, there really isn't a safe glasses option for dogs. Have your dog's vision checked at least annually. If your Miniature Goldendoodle is showing signs of deteriorating eyesight, make more frequent checkups so that you can adjust to help your dog better navigate around the home and on walks.

● Kidney disease is common in older dogs, and an ailment that you really need to watch for in your aging Miniature Goldendoodle. If your pup is drinking more often and having regular accidents, this could be sign of something more serious. Get your dog to the vet as early as possible if you notice this problem.

Nutrition

With less exercise, your Miniature Goldendoodle isn't going to require nearly as much food. If you feed your Miniature Goldendoodle commercial food, make sure that you buy the food specifically for senior dogs. You will want to reduce the calories without diminishing the taste, so you should plan to add some natural food to your dog's meals.

If you make your Miniature Goldendoodle's meals, you will need to make sure that you reduce the fat content. Increase the amount of lean meat you add. This not only helps keep the calorie count down and provide great taste, it also offers more protein. Don't use fatty meats, as that will hurt your dog more than help.

Exercise

Exercise gets trickier as a dog ages, particularly if he or she is accustomed to going out in the woods, hiking, or just romping in open areas. Your Miniature Goldendoodle may feel a little down as he or she can't do the things that were always so enjoyable. You will need to find other ways to interact and keep your canine happy, which is still fairly easy considering he pretty much just wants to be with you. You can keep training, but finding low-key activities that are just playing should be more than enough to keep your dog happy. Getting toys that are easy on your dog's teeth and playing games with him will keep your Miniature Goldendoodle active without overexertion.

It is very likely that your dog will start to gain weight. You will need to be particularly careful to make sure that the problem is not the presenting of a thyroid condition, but odds are it is just that you need to adjust your dog's diet. Of course, it could be that you are simply not making sure your dog is exercising enough. As long as your dog doesn't exhibit signs of pain or discomfort, make sure you keep the activities up, just for shorter durations.

Walks are still something your Miniature Goldendoodle can enjoy, but the walks will just need to be shorter and more frequent. Walks will be shorter distances, but probably will last nearly as long as your dog will sniff everything. Let your dog do this because he is moving at a more comfortable pace. As tempted as you may be to pick your dog up, don't. Take the time to enjoy your surroundings instead of getting annoyed at the slow pace and frequent stops. It is a new type of curiosity for your dog, and he or she is finally stopping to smell the roses (or blades of

grass and leaves). This is fine and can be just as enjoyable as those boisterous walks with a puppy.

Mental Stimulation

Though your dog may have slowed down, he or she is still a very
smart pooch, so you can start to change physical activity for more mental ones. Playtime can be more puzzle solving, and you can keep training
them. There is no such thing as a dog that is too old to train, especially
for the more intelligent breeds. Since their walks are for shorter distances, this is the perfect way to supplement the mental stimulation they
used to get through physical activities. Fetch can be traded out for hide
and seek, and your Miniature Goldendoodle will be more than happy to
hunt for you as a way to play.

Photo Courtesy Of
Kristin Piltz

Regular Vet Exams

Photo Courtesy Of
Wandalyse Worrell

Regular vet visits are essential for senior people and senior dogs. It isn't necessarily because of problems, but wellness checks should be more often just to make sure your dog is all right. Your vet can let you know if your Miniature Goldendoodle is either too active or not active enough given the dog's weight and current physical abilities. If your canine is injured and tries to hide that from you, your vet is much more likely to notice.

Your vet can also make recommendations about activities and your Miniature Goldendoodle's schedule. For example, if your canine has begun to pant more, this could be a sign of pain caused by stiffer joints or something else. Changing the walks or how you play can help ease the pain. Your vet is a fantastic resource for getting a more physically comfortable range of activities during the later years of your little guy's life.

Potential Old-Age Aliments

Chapter 17 covered the most problematic ailments for Miniature Goldendoodles, and many of these will not show up until the later years. In addition to hereditary diseases, old age comes with its own sets of ailments that are pretty universal across the canine world, such as arthritis. Be more aware of your Miniature Goldendoodle's behavior because this could indicate that your dog is not as healthy as you think. Some symptoms could be caused by the aging process, while others could be a sign of something more serious. Monitor your Miniature Goldendoodle and set up appointments if you notice anything that seems strange or see a shift in your Miniature Goldendoodle's personality.

Regular grooming is also important because you can see potential issues. Since Golden Retrievers do have skin conditions, you want to make sure your dog is comfortable in the older years, so you will need to brush your pup more often. Having established regular brushings, teeth care, and washings, you will be able to spot issues that could indicate a problem. Your Miniature Goldendoodle's breath may get worse, which could be a sign of gum disease. Skin infections may be worse, requiring a change in shampoos, your brush, or something else. The bond you formed all of those years ago through brushing is definitely a help now to keep your aging friend healthier longer.

Enjoying The Final Years

Your Miniature Goldendoodle's senior years can be amazing and incredibly enjoyable because your small companion will be a real couch potato. After a long day or when it is really rainy, don't feel guilty about not being able to go for a long walk. Turn on the TV and gently play with your Miniature Goldendoodle on the couch. Do a short training session of all the old familiar tricks, then kick back with a book. It is an incredibly mellow time that can make life a lot easier, while giving you a bit more time in your schedule. Puppies require nearly all of your time; senior dogs just need you around for cuddling.

Steps And Ramps

If your dog is smaller, you may be tempted to pick up your Miniature Goldendoodle when you reach stairs and steps. Fight that urge because it is not helping your dog. By carrying your dog, you are speeding up the deterioration of your dog's muscles, meaning the dog's body will be less capable. That doesn't mean you should expect your canine to go up and down long flights of stairs daily, but don't pamper your pup for small staircases and easy-to-maneuver steps.

You should have ramps around your home and in your car so that your dog can continue to do the basic activities without assistance. The ramps will need to be wide enough that your dog doesn't fall off of them. Someone should always be present and near the dog as he or she goes up and down the ramp. That way your pup has a spotter in case his or her balance is off or there is a misstep.

Enjoy The Advantages

Miniature Goldendoodles are one of those breeds of dogs that are just as much fun in their senior years as when they are pups—perhaps more if you aren't into training from scratch. They tend to retain that fun-loving, carefree attitude that draws people to them. They are people pleasers just as much in their later years as in the early ones. If you want to train, they are game. If you want to kick back, just lend them your lap or a place right beside you. About the only real change is that the walks will have to be shorter and long hikes are out of the question, but if you go out more often, that may be just as welcome since it forces you to take breaks more frequently.

It is even possible that your Miniature Goldendoodle will start to initiate relaxing sessions. He may let you know he just wants to get on the couch and chill if he isn't feeling up for real activity. Because he or she is able to pick up on your social cues, he may know just want you need, convincing you to rest no matter how busy you are. After all, if your best friend needs to rest on the couch, how can you say no?

What To Expect

Your Miniature Goldendoodle probably isn't going to suffer from fear that you are less interested in spending time with them. He or she will continue to be the happy, friendly companion you have always loved, but with more limits than in previous years. Your Miniature Goldendoodle's limitations should dictate interactions and activities. If you are busy, make sure you schedule time with your Miniature Goldendoodle to do things within those limitations. Your happiness is of utmost importance to your Miniature Goldendoodle, so let the little canine know you feel the same way about his or her happiness. It is just as easy to make an older Miniature Goldendoodle happy as it is to make a young one happy, and it is easier on you since relaxing is more essential.

Made in the USA
Columbia, SC
13 November 2020